True Stories From A Policeman's Notebook

by

Turk Parker

So, you think you want to be a cop, do you? Then come along on patrol with me.

Big-city cops often have ten or twenty adventures in a single night's shift. You'll go from one desperate call for help to another, until your uniform is soaked with sweat.

And that's the way these stories are written: stark, uncensored, and just the way they happened in cruel reality.

Like the lives they record, these stories are nasty, brutish and short.

So put on your uniform and step into our patrol car.

Snap your seat belt on, partner. You're going to need it.

TABLE OF CONTENTS

Rachel

Despite her parents' shouted pleas to God to let them die instead of her, the baby stopped breathing.

I had other terribly mournful calls, but none were sadder than one I had out in the Sunnydale projects.

The Sunnydale is a group of poured concrete housing projects in the southern part of San Francisco, built on the theory that if you can concentrate all the welfare recipients in one area, you can take care of their housing problems economically, without disturbing influential taxpayers with the welfare recipients' miserable existence.

On this particular night, we got a call of a baby who had stopped breathing, and we went to the house where it had occurred. The radio dispatchers generally sent the police out on every ambulance call in the Sunnydale, because the ambulance crews were reluctant to go into the projects without an armed escort.

We had no trouble finding the house. We didn't even have to look for the house numbers. We could hear the family crying in grief from over a block away.

The ambulance crew arrived with Mercury heels. The paramedic snatched up the baby in his arms, and sprinted, full tilt, out the door to the ambulance.

But the possibility of a miraculous medical intervention was not thought by the family to be at all likely, and they were already deep into mourning.

The infant's mother was laid out on the only couch in the house, because she was unable to stand. This was her second child to be born—and her second child to die. Her first baby had been killed in an auto accident. Other family members stood around, as stricken as cherubs in Giotto's *Lamentation*, and as one, they wailed in a spontaneous, rhythmic choir of grief.

She was an attractive woman, of about thirty. Her eyes were red from weeping. Her husband hovered over her, whispering words of comfort and love, like a muscular protecting angel. He looked up at us, with an expression of hopeless suffering.

Their pastor arrived. The role of churches in the black community is far more important than the role the churches have had in white communities since the end of the Middle Ages. In the days of slavery, churches were the only organizations black people were allowed to have, and all their needs had to be filled by those churches—the black pastor is a community leader of far greater power than his white counterpart. He is that community's spokesman, adviser on all matters, director of community opinion, almost a government unto himself, and a figure of authority whose presence is required at every important event.

The pastor was a short man with slicked back hair, wearing a dark suit with an impossibly white starched shirt. He began a dirge, quoting from Jeremiah, "Before I formed you in the womb, I knew you…" and after every sentence he spoke, the family and friends responded with a unison of tearful sobs.

He spoke—actually, it was more of a song—of how this baby was loved by God from before the beginning of the world. Each time he stopped to draw a breath, his words were answered with moans from the assembled group, who then were silent when he delivered his next sentence. The rhythm of the dialogue of grief was both inexpressibly sad, and incomprehensibly beautiful.

We left that breathing rain of tears and went to the next call for help, of which there was never any shortage in the Sunnydale. I didn't want to handle anybody's burglary, though. I just wanted to sit somewhere and cry. I couldn't do that. I had to just go to the next call for help, with my heart dead inside me.

But I soon learned that I was to reenter that unhappy maelstrom of weeping, because I received a call from the Operations Center to go back to the house, and tell the parents that their baby was dead.

My partner and I drove back to the house. I did not imagine that in another two decades, I would trade places with that sorrowing family, when I was to hold my own beautiful, doomed son as his life bled out of him. But the baleful nightmare that was to stalk my life was not yet devouring my psyche, and I had no premonition of its fell footsteps behind me.

We walked up to the door. The house was full of people, so full that the crowd was standing outside the front door, unable to enter. Our arrival brought an immediate hush in the crowd outside, which spread to the gathering inside, like a silent telegraph message of dread anticipation.

With each of our steps, the crowd parted.

This poor family had no job, no education, no car, no money—but they had hoped for the future, and they had two wonderful children, only to see them both snatched by death. And now they had nothing.

No one made a sound as we approached the tearful parents through the close-packed gathering, which drew back from us in horror as if we were the very Angels of Death. They saw in our faces our grave purpose.

We took off our uniform hats, and held them to our chests. The two parents looked at us with grief and terror at what they knew we would say.

"I am very sorry," I said. "I regret to tell you that your baby has died."

We turned and left through the silent crowd, and as we stepped through the door, we heard the chilling sound of a single keening voice, calling out to God.

It was the dead baby's mother, weeping for her children and refusing to be comforted, because her children are no more.

Aftermath

A very bad thing happened to my friend—a very bad thing indeed, and it didn't help at all that we all considered him a hero.

He was a short, stocky man, and we were both young cops working in the Potrero district of San Francisco. He loved police work. It was adventure, play, fun, companionship—things we love about policing.

His hobby after work was going on dates with women about whom it would be a compliment to say that they were half-human. His favorite fishing hole for such adventures was a saloon called the Horse and Cow, a joint that catered mainly to submarine sailors, and which was on San Francisco's Third Street, but which has since moved to Martinez.

The devil's brew of trouble which was served up at the Horse and Cow may be sampled by an incident which took place one night. A lithe young brunette entered the bar and was accidentally over-served. She picked up two sailors, and invited them home.

Walking with the pair of mariners to her apartment, she began to sober up, and realized that she may have bitten off a little more than she could chew.

Her solution to this problem was to walk into the middle of the street and scream for help. The police arrived, determined that the salts had done nothing illegal, and sent them back to their boat. The cops offered the young woman a ride home. She said nothing, but took off her dress and put it on the hood of the radio car.

The dress and a pair of stiletto heels were the entire inventory of her clothing. She did a little dance, stark naked, in front of the car, with the whole neighborhood looking on. The coppers arrested her, and tried to put her into the prowl car. She fought like fifty wildcats, and once she was in the back of the car, she proceeded to kick out the windows with her high heels.

I was in the Black Mariah that night, so when the cops on the scene called for a wagon, it fell to me to respond. We put her in the back of the bread wagon, kicking and screaming. In those days, women did not have tattoos unless they were either employed by a circus, or were trying out for Homecoming Queen of the Hells Angels. She had a tattoo on each cheek of her behind: on one side was "UL Tested," and on the other was the "Good Housekeeping Seal of Approval."

We got to the City Prison, and the guard at the door asked why I had her dress in my hand. I said that she took it off, and was fighting so hard we were afraid to uncuff her.

Sometimes, guys in this business get pretty salty, and after a few years, they think they can handle anything.

That is not always the case.

The guard had probably been a policeman when I was in kindergarten, and he thought he was pretty tough.

He said, "Kid, I can handle her. Take off her cuffs, so I can get the dress on her." She flashed an "I am Woman, hear me roar" smile of the sort you see in divorce courts when spousal support is handed out, so I knew things were about to end badly. I said to watch out because she was dangerous.

The guard snorted in contempt, and said, "Kid..." But that's all he said, because as I released the cuffs, she decked him with a right cross that had the swift potency of a rattlesnake bite.

Naturally, she had dated my friend—several times.

My friend's amorous adventures strained his budget, so he took a part-time job as a bank teller. Banks frequently hired cops as tellers in the hopes that they would catch robbers.

One day, my friend was in the bank bathroom, when two robbers came in. They both had guns. They knew the bank had a police teller, but they didn't know what he looked like. They demanded to know who the cop was. It was their plan to shoot him first, and then rob the bank. But everybody covered for him, and said he wasn't there.

At that moment, my friend emerged from the bathroom, reading a novel, in his civilian clothes indistinguishable from any other customer. He saw the situation, but pretended to be absorbed in his reading, and went out the front door.

If you pretend you're doing something very important, other people take your cues and treat you the way you show them to treat you. It's as if you're writing a play, and assigning roles to people—and they spontaneously act as the characters you have assigned to them. In this case, he ignored the robbers, read his novel, and they didn't stop him as he went out the door.

There, he took up a position behind a parked car, and with a huge automatic in his hand, he waited for the robbers.

The robbers emerged from the bank and ran across the street. My friend told them to stop. They both shot at him.

This was a serious error. Unless you have been practicing, it is very difficult to hit anything with a handgun, except by chance. They missed my friend.

But my friend had been practicing, all right, and he shot back. He did not miss. He shot one robber in the face, and winged the other. One robber was dead, the other was in custody, and we all considered my friend to be a hero.

I told him that when I saw him the next evening, and he said, "Oh, yeah, thanks." But he had a look of indescribable suffering.

There was one thing I was quite unprepared for in police work, and that was the effect that killing a suspect has on police officers. I grew up with movies and TV shows in which the cops kill the robbers, and there is nothing afterwards to indicate that this is a traumatic event: no discussion of the fact that the cop has taken a human life, no tears, no sleepless nights, no investigations, no demonstrations, no alcoholism, no nightmares, no stress, no divorces, not even any paperwork. But in real life, there is a price to be paid when you take a human life, any human life, even the life of a robber who is trying to kill you—and that price is high. My friend was the first person I knew before and after a shooting. It was the first time I saw a happy-go-lucky guy turned into a miserable, depressed wretch. But it was not the last time I saw that happen.

People in this country act as if taking human life is no big deal. I assure you, it is a big deal. No matter what the life, no matter what the circumstances, it is a very big deal. The enormity of a killing cannot be described in words.

My friend stopped going to the Horse and Cow. He stopped going out at night. He stopped telling jokes, or even smiling. He finally went to the Captain, and said, "I can't stand this job any more." He gave the Captain his star and his gun, and signed a resignation.

Crucifixion

All the other cops thought that Jack Young should have been a priest instead of a policeman. He was a quiet, unassuming guy, given to wearing black sweaters that hid his sergeant's stripes, and always helping people just at the right moment.

He was a saint, no doubt about it. We all liked him, and admired him. People stopped swearing when he was around, not because he even asked them to, but just because they didn't want to fall below his standards. People would talk about things with him, personal things, and they would follow his gentle advice. Usually, his advice made things turn out pretty well.

To a Christian, a saint is somebody who shows heroic sanctity, someone who reflects Christ in a way that is especially close, someone who shows kindness, and wisdom, and does good things, and maybe, in a few instances, suffers or dies while he is doing those good things. What counts is how you live, not how you die, because you only die once, but it's a real plus for a saint to die doing good things. It's like graduating Summa Cum Laude for a saint to die in a way that resembles Christ's crucifixion, like St. Olaf did for the Vikings, dying in a battle against impossible odds, an act that converted the Vikings, or St. Peter getting crucified in Rome. But most saints, like most people, die in bed, and we look at their lives as a whole.

To Jack Young, being a policeman was his way of imitating Christ. He used every opportunity to do good works.

I got to know him because of his response to poverty—my poverty. I was a Police Cadet, kind of a Fascist Piglet, while I was in college, and every single dime of my salary went to the ravenous maw of my college Bursar's Office. I lived in my parents' home, saving money every way I could.

My poverty came to Jack Young's attention in a roundabout way, because of a girl.

I was always trying to devise ways to take girls out on dates without spending the money I didn't have. A free concert came up, and I thought it was an excellent chance to ask out a really lovely young redhead, gorgeous of face and form. She had great big eyes and a glowing complexion—just a radiantly beautiful young woman, and to my delight, she said yes. She was an identical twin, and I previously had the impression that when you spend genetic material on two people instead of one, the people should come out faded, like a rubber stamp you use on two papers. But not this girl: she was as beautiful as two Miss Americas put together. She was about a fourteen on a scale of ten.

But when she perceived that this was going to be a cheap date, she kind of soured. The date ended early. I felt as if I had gone to the gates of Paradise, close enough to almost taste indescribable happiness, and had been sent away, into the outer darkness, where there is weeping and gnashing of teeth.

In the self-loathing postmortem introspection of the experience, I realized that spending money on a girl is an important part of a good date: you have to show her that she is worth spending money on, and you have to show her that you are at least potentially a good provider. There was no easy solution to my problem, however, because I didn't have time for yet another job, and I had to pay tuition. So I hit on the idea of asking my parents for lunch money, and then not eating lunch. After two or three weeks of hunger, I could ask a girl out, and it wouldn't be an embarrassing situation. (Not the redhead, mind you. She wouldn't talk to me after that.)

Jack Young noticed that I didn't eat lunch. Now, normally, only women notice things about other people. Men don't usually have that kind of interest in other people. By the time a man takes the same notice in other people that an ordinary woman takes, that man is practically a saint. But Jack noticed that I didn't eat lunch at work, and without making any embarrassing inquiries, he mentioned to me that his wife always packed too much for him to eat, and said he was trying to lose weight—a matter that was much more obvious to him than to me—and would I help him out by consuming half a turkey sandwich. This became a regular thing. He even gave me advice on girls, which usually worked out pretty well, but not on the redhead—he was a police sergeant, after all, not a magician.

Then, one day, the Chief announced that Jack Young was going to be transferred from an administrative job to Ingleside Station, where he would be a street supervisor. Jack had a bad heart. We all thought he'd die of a heart attack, because of the stress. Some patrolmen even went into the Chief's office and berated him for doing something we just knew would kill Jack.

Unless you've been in an organization like the Army or the Police Department, you don't know what an extraordinary thing that was. The police organization is built on discipline and obedience, and for patrolmen to go to the Chief and tell him off is just unheard-of. But they did it.

They did it to no avail. Jack Young went to Ingleside. People told him he should retire, which he could have done, so he wouldn't die. But he said being a policeman was what he wanted to be, and he would show everybody that he would do what he was supposed to do. This was his life; this was the way he did good works. He wanted to set an example. So Jack went to Ingleside.

But the people who thought Jack's heart would give out were wrong. He didn't die of a heart attack at all.

Instead, he died because someone walked into Ingleside Station, pointed a shotgun at Jack's chest, and pulled the trigger.

Boxer

Prizefighters and prostitutes sacrifice their health for the amusement of others. People expect them to enjoy their work, or at least not to complain, and to pick themselves up and carry on after each new trauma. People allow themselves such amusements at the expense of others because they do not truly regard boxers and whores as human beings like themselves. People regard them in much the same way that people might say, "That's their job, and they expect that" about soldiers or policemen who are killed in the line of duty. It is as if they were machines instead of some mothers' children.

He was a boxer.

Knowledgeable boxing fans might correct me to say that he was a fighter, because to them, a boxer is someone who scientifically defeats an opponent, dodging the blows that are meant to knock him down, and my friend never did that. He stood up and took whatever blows came his way, with no thought to avoiding them. He was successful in the ring because he could ignore the blows, pick himself up and hit back, and when he hit back, his opponents often found themselves looking up from the canvas.

He was born and raised in the ghetto, and he stayed there, even when he became a ranked Middleweight prizefighter, and world famous. He was known as a tough opponent, ready to take a hit and give a hit. Dodging away from a punch was not his style.

He was successful, and as he worked his way up through the Middleweight ranks, he became famous. Everyone knew him, and he was a likeable guy. But in the upper ranks of boxing, it is not enough to just be a fighter. The very best boxers can dodge your fists, so your punches land in thin air, and then they come back at you, and put their fists in your face with enough force to make you forget your name.

The human brain is floating in fluid inside the skull, and it is about the consistency of Jell-O. It is not meant to be pounded against the skull, and that is what happens to it when a boxer is hit in the face.

No matter how brave you are, or how manly, or how strong, there comes a time when your brain cannot take too many more traumas, and that is what happened to my friend. As he worked his way up the ranks, he met boxers who could dance away from him and then hit him in the face, and he started to lose.

Somehow, he had the sense to get out of the ring, and he was able to get a job as a Federal housing policeman, working in the same Federal housing projects that he grew up in. He was loved, and respected, and feared. He was very happy in that job.

The blows to the head he had suffered in the ring caused him problems. It was sometimes difficult for him to talk, and his eyes were going bad. But he was working as a housing policeman, and that was enough.

Late one night he was riding through the Sunnydale projects with a Sergeant beside him, when he spotted a stolen car, and followed it into a cul-de-sac. As soon as the car came to a stop in front of the projects, a lot of young toughs surrounded the police car, and the Housing Police Sergeant called for a backup.

My partner and I were about three blocks away, and we drove hell bent for leather to help them out. But in the few seconds it took us to get there, the situation had changed. The Sergeant had one young thug against a car, and he was banging on him with his flashlight. Two of the local Philistines were running away for dear life. Two more men were on the ground unconscious near the Boxer, and one man was literally on his knees begging for his life. When we arrived, he screamed at us to save him from the Boxer. The Sergeant said that as soon as they were attacked, the Boxer became an awesome god of war, flattening his opponents one after the other.

The Boxer was quite popular with the ladies, too, and he regarded the projects as his own personal harem. His reputation as the Alpha Male of the district was enhanced with every story we heard, and every experience we had.

He was a fast worker in the romance department, too. One night, we got a call of a family fight. A woman called that her live-in boyfriend had come home drunk and was abusive. My partner and I arrived at the door, with the Boxer following us as backup. The woman answered the door, stark naked, and pointed to the stairs: "He's up there. He hit me. I want him to go to jail." So we went up the stairs.

After we got the handcuffs on the boyfriend, I looked around for the Boxer. Neither he nor the woman could be seen. I sent my partner downstairs to see if the Boxer was all right, and in a moment he returned, laughing.

He whispered in my ear, "He's down there, all right. With her. And her nipples are *wet*."

A few weeks after that, a drunken bus driver ran his bus into a tree. The Boxer was the first cop on the scene, and the bus driver, a giant of a man who towered over the Boxer, did not like having a policeman tell him to get out of his bus—so he took a swing at my friend. This was not an act of good judgment. The Boxer's mind went to off, and his fists went to on, and the bus driver had to be taken to the hospital in an ambulance on a stretcher.

But the Boxer's injuries caused him problems. He couldn't remember things, and it was hard for him to speak coherently—and these problems got worse. He left the Housing Police job, and for a while he did odd jobs.

Then some fight manager convinced him that he could have a second chance at the Middleweight crown. We were afraid for him, because we knew that he would just take hit after hit, courageously ignoring his pain, and he couldn't afford to take too many more hits. We heard news reports of his fights: knockout after knockout as he advanced steadily up the Middleweight ranks—and then, when he met truly good boxers, several crushing defeats. He always picked himself up and wanted to go on fighting, but eventually the referees stopped the fights, and finally even the boxing doctors refused to pass him on his boxing license medical tests. His boxing career was through.

I met him once more. He was working as a security guard in a supermarket. His walk was unsteady, and when I greeted him, I had to tell him my name. I stuck out my hand, and he tried to take it to shake it, but at first he missed. I realized that he was nearly blind. We talked about the good old days, about our adventures as policemen in the ghetto. He smiled, his scarred lips parting to show several missing teeth. "Yeah, we had fun," he said, laughing. "Life is good."

Captain

It was everybody's opinion that the Captain was the smartest human being in the entire Department, and that he would be Chief, except for his fatal flaw.

I came to know the fatal flaw at about three one morning, when as a rookie cop I had to put my Captain into a jail cell.

The Vietnam War was just winding down, and many soldiers coming back from the war had become radicals and used the skills that they had learned in the Army to shoot at policemen. We were very often getting shot at in my station, which was out by the Hunters Point ghetto.

On this particular night, I was the book man—I was in the station, and my duty was to keep a log book of all the events in the district. The only other person in the station was the Lieutenant.

The Lieutenant was at the end of his career, and a more cynical Norseman I never knew. He typically spent the evening smoking cigarettes from a long black cigarette holder with a filter in it to keep himself from getting lung cancer, and writing poetry in a little spiral notebook that he kept. He had been in the Marines during the Second World

War, and he was delighted when the Federal prison at Alcatraz Island shut down, because they had Thompson sub-machine guns which they gave to the San Francisco Police Department. He had carried a Tommy gun in the Second World War. He always kept the Tommy gun that had been assigned to the station in his upper right-hand desk drawer, just in case the station were attacked. On most nights, he was the only one in the station who ever wanted to have the Tommy gun nearby. The only exception was on Easter morning, when we all went up onto Hunters Point hill to watch the sunrise, and at the very break of dawn, we used to let off a few rounds from the Thompson.

But this was not Easter, and the Thompson was in the Lieutenant's drawer.

We heard a scratching at the back door. The back door was made of armored steel, with a small bullet-proof glass window. I looked out the window, but I couldn't see anything. I went back to the book.

The Lieutenant heard the scratching again, and we decided that we might be under attack. He took out his Tommy gun, and I cranked a round into the chamber of the station shotgun. We made a plan between us that he was to throw open the door, and I was to empty the shotgun at whoever was on the other side, and then the Lieutenant would finish off the attackers with the Thompson. Looking back on it now, I can see that there were certain potential defects in this plan, but it seemed like a good idea at the time.

The Lieutenant threw open the door and there in the dim light, looking down the barrel of my 12 gauge and up at the readied Tommy gun, was the Captain. He had been lying on the ground with his head on the door. When we opened the door, his head fell on the floor. The Captain was in full uniform, including his gold braided hat, and he was so drunk that he couldn't stand up. He had crawled in full uniform from the bar across the street, across four lanes of traffic to the station. He had peed in his pants. He looked up at me over the barrel of my shotgun and said, "Young officer, get me my car keys. I'm going home."

His reasoning was evidently that he had to drive because he was too drunk to walk, but somehow we didn't think that was a particularly good idea.

We had a couple of prisoners in the station jail cells, and the Lieutenant declared instant amnesty. I gave them their property back, told them that today was their lucky day, and ushered them out the front door of the station. Then the Lieutenant and I carried the Captain, who had lapsed into unconsciousness, into a cell, took away his gun, and locked the cell door.

I was completely horrified by the situation. I was a rookie cop, and I could be fired at any time. If I were to become permanent after the end of my rookie year, it would only be after my Captain had recommended me. And I had just put the man on whom my job depended into jail. I didn't feel good about this situation at all.

I was astounded at the attitude of the Lieutenant, who seemed completely unperturbed by the incident. He was a very cool character. After we put the Captain in the jail cell, the Lieutenant put his Tommy gun back in his desk drawer, lit another cigarette in his long holder, and went back to writing poetry. I resolved that if I ever got to be a Lieutenant, I would always try to be as calm in a crisis as he was.

After a couple of hours, we opened up the cell, and saw that the Captain was snoring loudly. The Lieutenant got the key to the door of the Captain's office, and we carried him into his office. When he woke up in the morning, he was sitting in his office chair, and he never gave us any indication that he remembered what we had done.

Despite his fatal flaw, we generally liked working under his command. The reason was that he very often used his quite superior intelligence to keep us out of trouble —or at least to keep us from the consequences of the trouble that we did get into.

Like a lot of people with superior abilities, he liked to rub his intelligence in other people's faces. People like to feel superior, so if they have an ability that other people don't have, they like to humiliate people by demonstrating how superior they are. We didn't like his attitude, but we did like the fact that he would try to keep the Chief downtown from finding out anything that we had done which might be improper.

For example, one night one of the guys shot a telephone.

In those days, we were always being shot at, and the midnight watch falling in looked like the National Guard going out on maneuvers. Everybody had a rifle, except me and one other guy. I carried an artillery model Luger, which was a German substitute for a rifle, the longest pistol I could get my hands on, and the other guy carried a grenade.

One of the crew who had a rifle was unloading it in the locker room, and for some reason it went off. We were kind of upset about it, not merely because this endangered us all, but also because it is simply unprofessional. There shouldn't be any reason for an accidental discharge of a weapon. In this case, the rifle was an AR-15, which was the civilian version of the rifle that the officer had carried in Vietnam. We ragged on him a little. We liked him a lot, and we didn't want anything bad to happen to him, but this was something for which he was simply going to have to take some ribbing.

The bullet had gone across the locker room and had destroyed a telephone hanging on the wall. When the gun went off, everyone in the locker room just froze in horror. The Sergeant on duty, no fool, went to the bottom of the stairs leading to the locker room and shouted up, "Is everything all right up there?" Naturally, we all said that everything was just fine. The Sergeant did not want to know of anything that might constitute trouble. Then he would have to make a report about it, and explain why he hadn't prevented it. It was much better, in his view, that he didn't know about it.

So we had a rifle bullet through a telephone, and we had to make sure that nobody else found out. We immediately got in our patrol cars and went up and down Third Street until we found a telephone truck. We pulled over the poor telephone man with our red lights and sirens. "You fix telephones?"

"Yes, Officer."

"Do you fix wall phones?"

"Yes."

"Follow me to the police station."

We got the poor phone repairman to put in a new wall phone, and we gave him a good bottle of Scotch. Cops often have a bottle around because liquor is frequently given between cops as a "thank you" or as a substitute for money. Then we took the old wall phone to a taxidermist. We had it mounted on a taxidermist's plaque is if it were a deer's head: the handset became the horns, the bells became the eyes, and the dial was the mouth. We mounted this trophy on the wall near the new phone, just to yank the chain of the officer who had shot the phone.

We had no doubt that the Captain knew about this incident instantly. But if he *didn't* know about it, he wouldn't have to report it to downtown, and so he scrupulously avoided asking anyone any questions that we ever heard of. He was never on record as knowing about the rifle shot. He didn't want the Chief to think he couldn't control the cops in his station. He was observed asking a Sergeant one afternoon if anyone was upstairs in the locker room, and when the Sergeant said nobody was there, he went upstairs and came down again laughing. But he never said a word to any of us.

We figured that was worth a few times when we saw him drinking, and a few other times when he would torment us to show us how smart he was by asking us questions we could not answer. You had to stand there in front of him, while he cross-examined you about your knowledge of the law, or an arrest you might make, or any other matter that came to his mind. He just loved to torment his subordinates, showing everybody that he was smarter than they were.

In a lot of ways, we were all like monkeys in a cage at the zoo, twisting each others' tails for entertainment.

The Captain's immediate superior, supervisor, and nemesis was a stocky, take-charge, testosterone-filled individual, the Deputy Chief. He shaved his head bald even before it was popular. He took pride in being decisive. He loved to shout orders at people, even in an office. He despised the slender, intellectual Captain, and the feeling was mutual. In spite of his rudeness to subordinates, I respected him, because I sometimes had to call the Deputy Chief out of bed in the middle of the night for a decision on different crisis cases, and I always got a straight-up, reasonable decision.

In emergency situations, almost any reasonable decision will yield some positive results. Having an immediate, clear order to follow, even if it isn't an insight of genius, is much better than having a delayed decision that may ultimately be wiser, and it is far better than having no decision at all.

Generally I didn't care what the decision was, as long as I had an order from a superior officer to follow—but the Deputy Chief's orders were usually wise. And on those occasions on which, in the light of the next morning, the decisions turned out to be less than wise, the Deputy Chief always had the courage and the integrity not to deny that they were his decisions.

The Deputy Chief despised the Captain mainly for his drinking, and the Captain despised the Deputy Chief because the Captain despised everyone he thought was less intelligent than himself. That meant, of course, that the Captain despised just about everybody.

The Deputy Chief continually tried to catch the Captain drunk, and on one occasion thought he had the Captain nailed. He came in on the Captain, and observed eyes like red headlights. The Deputy Chief ordered the Captain to take a breath test—which the Captain refused. Instead, the Captain went to a doctor friend of his who certified that he was ill and under medication. The Deputy Chief tried to get him punished, but the Captain beat the rap.

Then it was the Captain's turn to get back at the Deputy Chief.

Throughout his career, the Captain had to spend time in various places of exile, whenever the Chief was displeased with him—which was frequently.

At this particular time, the Captain's Elba was Communications.

Rumor had it that the mayor was about to replace the Chief, and the Captain's name was being mentioned as a possibility, despite the general knowledge of his Achilles' heel. Everybody knew that the Captain was the smartest man in the Department. The Deputy Chief was likewise being considered.

When the mayor took a trip to China, the Captain struck back.

The Deputy Chief had a good friend who was a Sergeant in the Tac Squad. The Lieutenant in the Tac Squad was the Captain's friend. The Captain wrote a phony memo from one of the Captain's subordinates saying, "Captain, I am very sorry. The next time the mayor calls you from China, I will interrupt you no matter what you are doing. It won't happen again. And congratulations!"

The Captain had the phony memo Xeroxed, and a copy placed in the Tac Squad Lieutenant's inbox for just long enough for the Tac Squad Sergeant, who liked to know everyone else's business, to see it. The phony memo was then destroyed. Naturally, it took about thirty seconds for the Tac Squad Sergeant to report the contents of the memo to the Deputy Chief.

That day, the Deputy Chief visited the Captain about half a dozen times, trying to make up with him, and passing small talk: "Isn't it nice and sunny?" "Would you like to go to lunch?" "How about those Giants?" "The birds are sure chirping sweetly." The Captain was relishing every minute of this adulation, of course, and he enjoyed it even more later as the whole Department became aware of what he had done.

The Deputy Chief was furious—but there was nothing he could do. The Captain had shown himself to be smarter than the Deputy Chief—and that was what was most important to him.

We all want to feel superior. We want to think that we are good, intelligent, attractive, and powerful. Sometimes, the easiest way to feel good is to make other people feel bad, as if the way we feel should be relative to the way other people feel. People somehow think that if they are going to feel really good, other people have to feel really bad.

When we were children, we had to deal with bullies who punched us in the face. When we grew up, we had to deal with bullying in more subtle ways—people who dress better, or who let you know in front of other people that they went to a better school than you did, or that they drive a better car, or in any of a thousand other ways that they are better than you. We all love roses, and roses need manure. But these people delight in letting you know that they are the roses in life, and you are the manure. Adult bullies don't have to listen to Wagner and go goose-stepping around thinking they are better than other people in order to be bad to others. The boss who humiliates subordinates, the teacher who makes a cutting remark to a student in front of the class, the woman who gives the old stink eye to her husband because he was delayed in a traffic jam coming home—they are all bullies. They all feel better because you feel worse.

After he retired, I saw the Captain one more time. He had driven to the Hall of Justice, to get some papers. We talked for a while, and as he was leaving, I said I'd walk him to his car. He was parked in the basement of the Hall of Justice.

And so I knew that, somehow, the Captain had outsmarted everyone in the Department once again. Nobody but active-duty officers were allowed to parked in the basement of police headquarters—and even those parking spaces were at a premium, so they were restricted to those who had been given permits. There was a constant patrol to enforce that ban, and to tow away unauthorized cars. I couldn't wait to see what he had done.

In the basement garage of police headquarters, a section by the fingerprint lab was reserved for cars that had been towed for evidence processing by fingerprint technicians.

There, I saw the Captain's big Cadillac, with a handwritten note under the windshield wiper: "Do not touch! Hold for fingerprints!"

The Captain took the note from under the windshield wiper, and got in his Cadillac. He winked at me with a victorious smile, and drove off.

Cheerful

"When I die, I'm going to have some explaining to do," my friend told me, "So I have to be kind of careful now." My friend was always cheerful when he talked to me, and to have him speak of any negative subject was out of character for him.

"Explaining about what?" I was a Police Cadet, and my friend was a civilian Storekeeper who kept the inventory of property that the Department used, or seized. He worked by himself in a huge cave of a room in the basement of police headquarters. I was a little alarmed by his tone.

"Well, when I was younger, I did some things. For instance, when I was in the Navy, our ship docked in Hong Kong, and I went ashore, and I fucked a woman, and then I got drunk, and went across town, and fucked another one, both in the same day." He put both hands on his pot belly and chuckled a little bit. Then his face turned briefly into a scowl. "So I'm going to hell." His face alternated between a smile of remembered delight and a look of repressed horror at what he was going to face for it in the Hereafter, and back and forth a few times as his thoughts went from earthly paradise to spiritual perdition.

I thought I might give a little theological advice to lift his spirits. "Well, maybe not. Did you ever try confessing it?" Roman Catholics, like my friend and myself, believe in confession as a kind of rewind button on the videotape of life, able to delete parts of our life's tape that we think may cause us to wish for a suit of asbestos underwear later on.

"I'm not much for going to churches."

"Well, why go through life thinking you're going to burn? Confess what bothers you, and have done with it." Nobody likes confessing sins, but sometime we encourage each other, just for our mental health.

"When I pray, I like to do it alone. I don't like being with a lot of other people."

I knew that to be true. My friend was a short, heavy, bald man, and very shy. He knew me for about two years before he would talk about anything personal. The incident in Hong Kong was the first time he ever mentioned having a woman of any sort in his life at all. He lived alone. He was just too shy with people to have much success with women.

He had been a Chief Petty Officer in the Navy, and after he retired, he got a Civil Service job with the Police. He spent most of his time alone in a huge room full of police supplies. It suited him fine. He was a very shy person.

But he was also very cheerful, and kind to the people who met him. Although it was quite some time after I knew him before he would talk to me about anything but business, he was always happy to do anything for anyone. Whatever they requested, my friend was eager to do. So, to have him say that he felt frightened about his future was a concern for me.

In his time alone he liked to invent things; he gave me one of his inventions, which had actually been manufactured, a special kind of ruler with a curve on one end that allowed a typist to gauge how much room was left on a page for footnotes. People who do word processing on computers now have no idea of how difficult it was to figure out how much room to leave at the bottom of a page with a typewriter, and my friend had it solved. I used his invention constantly when I was in college.

He liked the Navy; it was like a family for him. My friend didn't have any family except one surviving brother, whom he called frequently. He always visited his brother on his vacation. His brother lived in the Midwest.

My friend's preoccupation was his stomach. Every lunch time, he took out a large skillet and fried up an enormous steak. He ate it with no vegetables or sauce or anything else that might get in the way of his enjoyment of the steak. I suspected that his breakfast and dinner menus were similar.

After I became his friend, my friend invited me to the old Naval base at Treasure Island, in the middle of San Francisco Bay, where there was a club just for noncommissioned officers—the NCO Club. He was as proud of it as a businessman might be proud of membership in some exclusive country club. He explained to me that it had much better food than the enlisted men's club, the same food as in the officers' club. "The only difference between the NCO Club and the Officers' Club is that the Officers' Club has tablecloths and higher prices!" he explained, smiling broadly and holding on to his pot belly. And it was very good indeed. Since my uncle had been a career Navy officer, I had been in the Officers' Club, where waiters in jackets served us on tables with tablecloths. But the food at the NCO Club was, just as he said, quite as good—and that was the important thing, as far as he was concerned. When we ate there, he was in heaven. He was almost always as cheerful a person as you would be likely to meet.

Now and then, though, his thoughts would turn to whatever sins he thought he had committed, and how he was going to burn for them. Roman Catholics believe that if you commit a mortal sin, which is the most serious kind of sin—usually, something you do with a woman, or stealing a very great amount of money, or committing suicide, for instance—you burn forever and ever. We used to think that eating meat on Friday was a mortal sin, because in the old days that was a church rule, and when I was in grammar school my schoolmates and I used to speculate on how many seven year old boys had enjoyed a hot dog at a Friday night baseball game, got clocked by a speeding truck on the way home, and spent the rest of eternity with the Devil. Later on in life, I came to think that this attitude must be really kind of insulting to the Creator who made the universe out of love, because it says that He (or, maybe She) is unjust. Justice is always proportional, and burning forever for a hot dog is not proportional. But when I was a child, such things escaped me.

Catholics used to make up a lot of sins that caused huge amounts of guilt and bad feelings, and I think the reason we did it is because we have the big safety valve, which is confession. Whatever it is you did, you can confess it, and then it becomes like kissing your sister—it doesn't count. So perhaps we tended to lay it on thick on the guilt side because the priest is in the forgiveness business, and ready to let us out of our well-deserved punishment. At least, that is the way it was explained to me when I was a kid.

But according to my friend, his transgressions were not kid stuff. He was an adult, and he had adult sins, and whatever they were, he was convinced that he would never see the face of God.

But the threat of that punishment could not get him to go into a church where there were all those people. He liked to be alone—but then, again, he didn't like to be completely alone. He talked to me frequently, and he was very close to his brother. Otherwise, he was content to stay by himself in the cavernous store room in the basement of the Hall of Justice, a solitary hermit meditating on his sins.

His brother's health began to fail, and my friend took time off to go back to see him. Then, one day, the news came that his brother had died. He was very upset, and flew back for the funeral. We were concerned, because his usual cheerful nature seemed to be absent. We knew how much he loved his brother.

A few days later, we got a call from the Midwest. It was the local sheriff saying that after the funeral, my friend went back to his brother's home, put his brother's shotgun in his mouth, and spread his brains onto the ceiling.

Laughing Boy

He was a sergeant, very intelligent, a teller of interesting tales and the sharpest wit within seven or eight police stations. It was a joy to have him around.

We used to call him "Laughing Boy." I'm not sure whether the name was originally meant to refer to the Irish hero Michael Collins, who was called "Laughing Boy" because he kept morale up so often when the Irish revolutionaries faced hard times —but it would have been appropriate. No matter how grim the cases we had to handle, he made us laugh, and he kept up a cheerful disposition.

There was a Captain who was widely hated, and thought to be mentally unstable. He humiliated the people working for him, yelled at them constantly in front of their coworkers, and had them working odd hours—some cops were starting their shifts at two o'clock in the morning. Any organization under his command quickly degenerated into the kind of place C. S. Lewis described in his brilliant account of Hell in *The Screwtape Letters:* a horribly nasty, incompetent bureaucracy full of back-stabbing and betrayal. If you set the interests of people against each other, it's not long before everybody is at war with everybody else, kind of like the saloon fights in the old-time cowboy movies where two people start fighting, and within ten seconds, everybody is fighting.

Laughing Boy, naturally, made up a phony transfer order sending that Captain to the station. Within a day, half of the officers in the station had submitted requests to be transferred out. The real Captain of the station, not knowing that the lunatic Captain was rumored to be transferring in as his replacement, was shocked: it is a terrible insult to a Captain to have half his men suddenly want to get out from under his command. Panic ensued until people got wise to the joke. Laughing Boy's reputation was well-established as a consummate practical joker.

He waited a few months before perpetrating his next outrage.

This was San Francisco, of course, where there is a politically powerful gay community, and every once in a while there was friction between the police and the gays. The police administration was always trying to think of ways to make us more understanding of gays, and to heal the rifts between the two groups. We had to attend classes, go on tours of homosexual and lesbian bars, listen to lectures, and otherwise go through mind-changing attempts by various experts in the field. Most of us thought it was a good idea to get along with other people, in general, but a lot of cops kind of resented the "in your face" attitude that they had to become politically correct and step into the shoes of people whose lifestyles they didn't share. And some people in the gay community were demanding that the cops watch gay pornography or visit gay sex clubs where they saw people stick things in various body cavities that you wouldn't think could possibly go there. Most of us didn't mind having a dinner, but a great majority really didn't want to watch a demonstration of the novel ideas some people had about sex. A lot of cops drew the line at that, and the hostility toward the political education classes grew.

Laughing Boy seized this opportunity for his next strike against the mental stability of the station. The torpedo he launched, which hit the station squarely amidships, was another phony order. Over a forged Chief's signature, the order said that in order to reduce the friction between the police and the transvestite community, officers were to take a special series of classes on transvestite issues. And to make the police more sensitive to the transvestite community, we all had to take the sensitivity training while wearing women's underwear.

The phony order said that the police uniform supplier had requisitioned a large supply of women's underwear, and everyone was going to have to go to the uniform shop to be issued women's underwear: bra, panties, fishnet nylons, and high heels, all in men's sizes. Everyone was going to have to stand for inspection before the sensitivity training classes while wearing the women's underwear, to make sure that no one failed to participate in this important community effort. Newspaper reporters had been invited to witness and photograph the event, so that a story about it would be properly disseminated to the community.

The uproar in the station was such that the Captain was called from home to quell the angry shouting and cursing. The Paris mobs in the French Revolution could not have been more dangerous, and had there been a guillotine handy, the Chief might have met the same fate as poor Louis XVI. But someone called a buddy in another station to ask how they were reacting to it, and it seemed a little strange that a Chief's order would just go to that one station. Finally, everyone realized that Laughing Boy had pulled another comic triumph.

Police work can be emotionally very difficult. Nobody ever got up in the morning and said, "What a wonderful day! The sun is shining, the birds are chirping, and I feel great! I think I'll call the cops." We only get called when things are in the toilet. And that wears on you: pretty soon, going from one tragedy to another, you get to be a sour, depressed grump.

Your moods are related to your thoughts. Bad moods are related to bad thoughts, and the bad thoughts you have are almost always untrue. Psychologists call the process of identifying bad, untrue thoughts and correcting them "Cognitive Therapy," and it is quite important in psychologists' efforts to cure depression. If you can think positive, happy thoughts, you will come to be in a positive, happy mood. And Laughing Boy, more than anyone else, tried to put everyone in a positive, happy mood. He was wonderful. His wit was always penetrating and sarcastic, but he deflated the stuffed shirts we hated, and raised our mood.

His masterpiece, however, involved the participation of several people from the station.

A drunk came into the station one night, and began cursing the Sergeant. He was put into a cell to sober up, but he wouldn't quietly go to sleep like most drunks—he spent four hours shouting and kicking the cell door so that the whole station resounded with the deep *bang, bang, bang* of a metal, barred door slamming against its jamb.

Finally, the drunk sobered up, quieted down, and was released. But the next night, he was drunk again, and noisy again, and the situation was repeated. This went on for about a week, and then Laughing Boy struck. He got everyone to participate in a little morality play.

One of the officers got dressed in civilian clothes, and pretended to be drunk. He was booked at the booking counter, cursing and screaming, and then he was put into the cell next to the noisy drunk, where he continued to scream curses and pound the door, just like the real drunk.

Another officer, with a gun loaded with blanks, came into the cell area and shouted at the officer pretending to be a drunk, "I've had enough of you! I told you this is the last time I'll take your abuse!" And he fired off the blanks at the officer pretending to be drunk, who fell to the floor in a loud, protracted dying scene, with catsup liberally spilled on the floor and his shirt. Finally, he lay still.

The drunk, for the first time, was quiet, looking with horror at the scene in front of him.

Then the Sergeant came in and saw the "dead" body. "Oh, my God! I've got to get the Lieutenant!"

So the Lieutenant came in, viewed the body and all the catsup, and said to the officer, "I thought I told you not to do this any more!"

The officer, looking penitent, said, "I'm sorry, Lieutenant, but he was cursing at me and I just couldn't stand it."

So the Lieutenant said, "Well, I suppose there's nothing to be done about it. Bury him out in the back with the rest. But ask my permission next time!"

Then the officer pointed to the problem drunk and said, "Lieutenant, he saw everything! What are we going to do with him?" By this time, of course, the drunk had peed in his pants with fright.

The booking Sergeant said, "Oh, he's all right, he's a regular guy. He won't tell."

The drunk said, "Oh, no! I won't tell! You'll never see me again. I'll leave town if you let me go." So they let him go, and the cops never saw him again.

But one of the officers who worked at the station, beloved of everyone, was killed in a gunfight.

After that officer was killed, Laughing Boy no longer told jokes, and he no longer wanted to come to work. We tried to raise his mood, but we were not sophisticated enough psychologists to know what was wrong.

Laughing Boy's moods darkened, permanently. He mourned our murdered companion, and nothing would take his mind off it. Finally, he told the Captain that he was retiring. We all encouraged him to stay, because we enjoyed his company so much. But he was having none of it.

"I hate this job," he said.

Vampire

It was a couple of nights before Halloween. I was working as a street Sergeant in the Taraval, and about quarter to four in the morning, we got a call of a man breaking into the basement apartment of a building near Sunset Boulevard.

I got to the scene, and there was another cop who arrived with me. We ran down the sides of the house, and saw no one, nor was there anyone in the backyard, nor the adjacent backyards, so we went to the door of the basement apartment and knocked.

The door was answered by a beautiful blonde in a little nightie and panties. I figured that this was another "Call 911 and make a policeman come" call, of which we got more than a few—but it wasn't.

She said that she had heard a prowler outside. We told her that we had checked the backyard and all the other backyards nearby, and nobody was there.

"Oh, thank God, Sergeant—but I know who it is."

"Who is it?" I said.

"It's Lestat the Vampire. I've been reading Anne Rice's book about him. Cats and dogs have been disappearing in the neighborhood, and I know it's him." I hadn't been expecting that answer.

But I decided to appeal to whatever was left of her rational consciousness. I said, "Madam, we would know immediately if people were showing up dead, drained of blood." She didn't seem to be high on drugs, or drunk. She was saying this cold sober, which was scary.

She looked at me like a schoolmarm at an errant pupil: "That's why vampires drink the blood of animals. Police don't investigate animal killings. It says so in the book. I was reading it, but it's too scary, so I had to stop and read something else."

She was really believing this, and I didn't know how to deal with it.

How do you know that Santa Claus—or even vampires—don't exist? In college, I'd had long discussions about this sort of thing. How do you know reality? Kant said we can never know the tree as a thing in itself, and Heisenberg said that observing things changes them—so how do we know reality? But I hadn't thought I'd have to deal with this question on a professional basis.

Some psychologists think that a lot of the things we perceive in the world are just imagined, like, perhaps, the Loch Ness Monster or Bigfoot. Carl Jung wrote a book on flying saucers, and what they mean psychologically. Some scientists think we project our thoughts on the world, and change the world.

I was not happy dealing with whatever thoughts this woman was projecting on the world.

Usually, children do not know when we are fooling them about Santa Claus, because the world is new to them, and the idea that there might be a Santa Claus is just as easy to believe as the idea that there might be gravity. G. K. Chesterton made a brilliant point about that in *Orthodoxy.* And it makes sense, when a genius like Chesterton writes about it. Why should there be gravity? Children might as well believe in Santa Claus as in gravity. There's no reason not to: we live in a magical universe. The earth exerts an unseen, unexplainable force that attracts things to it. Why should it? Just because we call it "gravity" doesn't make it any less magic, or any more understandable to scientists. Many adults have come to think of things like gravity as the way things ought to be, and nothing special at all, when it is really magic. They think of things like love and happiness as fairy tales, and not real—exactly the opposite of the way they ought to see them. *"Magic is something you don't understand,"* a Captain used to say to me during one of our discussions on the subject, and when I said, "What *is* magic, then?" he just repeated himself until I understood.

When they grow up, children come to understand that the world is often different from our beliefs about it. But beliefs color our understanding of the world, and even change the real world. Sometimes, people have very strange beliefs, and act on them. If enough people believe in a thing, they may even make a religion about it. I usually tried to avoid challenging people's magical beliefs, because of my rather cynical view that if they were able to accept such ideas as reality, there was no use dealing with them.

"Well, there's nobody in your backyard, and there's nobody in the adjacent backyards, so why don't you lock your doors and windows, and go to sleep?"

She was a nurse at U.C. Hospital. I could see her paycheck on the table. I hoped she didn't give me any treatment if I ever got sick.

She was getting exasperated with me. Obviously, the Police Department had sent her a fool. "Vampires can go through walls. Don't you know that?"

Evidently, I would have to bring up that gap in my education the next time I went to the Police Academy for training. "I forgot about that. Sorry." There are, in fact, vampires—people who feed off the lives of other people. There are a lot of them, actually. But they are psychic or emotional vampires, not the blood-sucking kind. If you are around one of them for very long, they will destroy you. They will tell you that you're no good, worthless, a failure, because they feel good if you feel bad. Pretty soon, you will come to believe it, and you will become a failure.

In this business, you learn to keep a straight face in all kinds of situations, and not react. But apparently I gave her a look that betrayed my feelings.

"You think I'm crazy, don't you? I'm not crazy. I have a friend." She picked up her telephone, and dialed a number. "Do you think I'm crazy?" were the first words out of her mouth to this friend, who apparently was not surprised to get such a question at four o'clock in the morning.

She looked at me with an air of triumph: "My friend doesn't think I'm crazy."

Inspiration came to me, and I asked if I could have the other officer take her to her friend's house to spend the rest of the night. That was all right with her, and with her friend, so she put on a coat over her nightie and panties, and went out the door. I was glad to be able to send her to her friend who didn't think she was crazy. I wondered what the friend was like.

The officer who was with me watched her prance out the front door in her high heels, and gave a big, lustful sigh. "I hope you don't mind driving her," I said. A man usually does a little mental calculation as to whether a beautiful but high-maintenance woman is worth the trouble, and I could see that he was wavering. She was gorgeous, but she was nothing but trouble, and he knew it.

The officer had his feet firmly planted in reality, even though he could see into her imaginary world.

He turned to me with a very sardonic smile and whispered, "I think I'll put some garlic on my dick."

Orphan

We found her at a bus stop, at about midnight. She was totally lost.

She was about thirty, well-dressed, with the distinctive eyes of Downs Syndrome.

She knew her name, but not her address. We checked the missing person files for anyone with her name or a similar description, and came up blank.

She had walked away from her home, and had been missing for about fifteen hours. This gave us two concerns: first, she was lost, and second, her family didn't seem to care enough to call the police.

It is not uncommon for mentally disabled people to be lost, and missing from home. What is unusual is for such a person to be missing for fifteen hours without anyone calling the police about it, and that was a bad sign.

When we got her to the police station, we sat her down in a comfortable chair, and she began to weep. We felt terribly sorry for her, and tried to cheer her up. We tried to get her to tell us what was wrong, but she wouldn't. We asked when she had eaten. She said she hadn't had anything all day, so we took up a collection among ourselves and sent a patrol car out to an all-night restaurant for a hamburger, fries and a chocolate shake. She ate these, and felt better—at least, better enough to tell us what was wrong.

She had lived with her parents up until a couple of years ago, when her mother died. She had been very close to her mother, who had cared for her in her home. They had loved each other deeply. Her father had been rather more distant, we gathered.

Her father was a retired businessman, wealthy, and with some real estate investments. About a year after her mother's death, her father met a much younger woman and married her. At first, her father's new wife pretended to love her and care for her, but now it was clear that the new wife wanted the retarded daughter to move out of the house.

When a spouse dies, and the remaining spouse remarries, it is certainly not uncommon to have conflicts between the new spouse and the children. Children want their parents to have an emotional bond, and when a new bride enters the family, children naturally feel that the surviving spouse is being in some way unfaithful. They feel threatened by the new wife. The new bride has to make some place of her own in the family, and that is hard, because she is displacing not only everyone who is still living, but also the ghostly mother whose status is sacred.

And there is another aspect which causes great trouble: children, especially adult children, perceive the father's new wife as someone who will grab their inheritance. The older the father, and the younger the bride, the more the children are likely to regard her not as a substitute mother, but as an unwelcome interloper who comes to take financial security from them, perhaps permanently.

Sometimes, that perception has no real foundation, and sometimes, the children's fears are justified.

We finally got enough information from the lost young woman to find out where she lived, and to talk to both her father and his new wife.

What we discovered from the conversations was alarming.

It was clear that the new bride intended to get this retarded daughter out of the house, and she didn't care how it happened or what befell the girl.

Children are always aware of the fact that their entire world depends on their parents, and children's tales are full of fears that their real mother will die and be replaced by a wicked stepmother. Carl Jung commented that such tales reflect people's reactions to different aspects of self, and to the different roles a mother plays. Sometimes, the real mother is both loving mother and wicked stepmother, in a child's eyes. But in this woman's case, the archetype had become reality, and it was a horrid reality, indeed.

This poor woman was living in a hideous Grimm Brothers fairy tale. She was stuck in a child's nightmare.

Now her mother was dead, and her father remarried, and her new stepmother didn't even want to live with her on the same planet. She was retarded, but she knew that she was the cause of the conflict, and that her father was likely to throw her out of her home in order to please his new wife.

We called for a social worker, hoping that would work some kind of domestic miracle.

We told her that we thought things might turn out well for her, after all. But she was having none of it. Her assessment of her situation was realistic and bleak: "I wish I were dead," she said.

A Regular Guy

He was a Sergeant when I was a rookie cop, and he was preparing to retire. He had been divorced many years before, and his family seemed to consist mainly of his elderly mother, for whom he provided support. He was very solicitous and loyal to his mother, because he knew that once she died, he would be pretty much alone. The thought did not sit well with him. He was a large, handsome man, an old-time Irish cop, with all the good things and bad things that might imply. Old-time Irish cops had a reputation for drinking, and corruption, and having a sympathetic heart to those who have a hard luck story.

Old-time Irish cops were reputed to drink, and the Sergeant was no exception. I never saw him drink on duty, which made him an exception in the old days, but he sure did like the sauce when he reported off. He'd get off the Midnight shift, and then report for duty at Fahey's saloon, where he patrolled the bar for a few hours before going home.

We liked him tremendously, and whenever the subject of his drinking came up, people made excuses for him: "He's a nice guy, and he just had a couple too many," or

"He needs to relax," and a thousand other reasons why it was OK for him to drink that way.

And true to the Irish culture, he was close to his mother, and he wanted to make sure he was there for her whenever she needed it. His mother was elderly, although quite active, and she always wanted the Sergeant to be careful. "I don't want to outlive you, you know," she used to tell him, and he always laughed at that, because there was not much chance of her outliving him.

He had a tremendous wit—a very sardonic, sarcastic sense of humor. Anyone who caused him to feel any displeasure was the subject of a comment that slid in between the ribs like a stiletto.

One night, I was his driver. In those days, Sergeants were regularly assigned a patrolman as a driver. The official reason was so that the two of us could take on criminals without waiting for a backup, but the real reason, most cops suspected, was so that a Sergeant could drink without the inconvenience of running the patrol car into a telephone pole. There were Sergeants who took advantage of that, but this Sergeant was not one of them. He drank heavily, but he drank off duty.

He was relaxing in the station office, when a call came over the air asking him to come to meet two cops who had made a traffic stop at 19th and Sloat.

He was displeased at having to go out of the station, because he was about to eat his lunch, but we got into the car and drove to meet the officers. On the way, I could tell that he was getting angry. He muttered to me, "These aren't rookies. These are two experienced cops, and they should know what to do without bothering me."

In the Police Academy, they had instructed us that when we went to the police stations, we should keep our eyes and ears open and our mouths shut, and that is exactly what I did. Unless you've been a cop for about five years, you really don't have enough experience to know what you are doing in most situations. Training and book-learning won't do it for you; you need to be in a thousand different situations to see how they are handled.

We pulled up behind the officers' patrol car, which had its red lights on, and there was a civilian car just in front of it.

One of the cops came over and talked to the Sergeant through the window. "Sarge, we pulled up behind this guy at the red light, and he was stopped. But when the light turned green, he didn't go forward, and the light changed to red again, and then green again, and he didn't move, so I went up to see what was wrong. He was asleep behind the wheel, and there's a bottle of whiskey beside him. So when I woke him up and asked for his driver's license, he handed me a ten dollar bill instead. What should I do?"

The Sergeant gave the officer a very pained expression, and asked, "What do you mean, what should you do?"

"I mean, should I arrest him for bribery?"

The Sergeant looked as if he had just stepped on a snail. He said, slowly, with great emphasis and the utmost contempt, "Oh, no, it's all right, he just thought you were a regular guy, that's all." And he motioned me to drive away.

We drove around for a while, and he had his arms folded. He was angry. I didn't say anything.

"Look here, kid," he said. When older cops called me "kid," I knew to keep my mouth shut. "Look here, kid," he repeated himself, "Never let me hear of you arresting somebody for bribery. You might not need the money, but the next cop might not feel the same way!" I just kept driving.

Then he said, to no one in particular, "Ten lousy bucks! That's a two hundred dollar fine. He could have offered ten percent at least!" I said nothing, and we went back to the station.

"I'm too old for this business," he said. "I think I'll put in my papers and retire."

He never did retire, though. One morning he stopped off at Fahey's bar after work, and had about half a dozen drinks to unwind. Then he tried to drive his car across the Bay Bridge, but found that he was unable to avoid steering into a massive steel support beam. Steel does not bend as people bend; "He's a nice guy, and he just had a couple too many" is not an argument that a bridge's foundation beam will accept as a valid excuse to suspend the laws of physics.

His mother found that she had outlived him, after all.

Kangaroo Court

He was an old-time beat cop on Sixth Street, and everybody liked him. Other cops enjoyed having him around. He was kind to everyone, and even the people he arrested spoke well of him.

It was suspected, but never proven, that sometimes he visited bars on his beat, and that the bartenders put something in a coffee cup for him that wasn't coffee.

How he came to be judged on this matter was something we all discussed for years afterward.

He was on the beat one afternoon, and he called in to Southern Station on the call box phone. He asked for a wagon to meet him, because he had arrested a kangaroo.

This was in the days before policemen carried small two-way radios, and the men on the foot beats had to call into the station every hour or so from one of the police call boxes scattered throughout the city. There was a telephone inside that rang at the station front desk.

The man at the station front desk was supposed to take the calls, and log them into a huge log book. He was the "book man." If a patrolman on a foot beat called in for a wagon, it meant that he had made an arrest and needed a patrol wagon to come to pick up the prisoner.

The book man took the call, but instead of making an entry in the log, he called the station Sergeant and whispered to him, "He's got the D.T.s! He says to send a wagon to Sixth and Minna because he's arrested a kangaroo!"

The Sergeant told the young officer, "Never you mind, my boy, I'll take care of it." And the Sergeant went to the Lieutenant.

In those days, beat men were notorious for drinking on the job, and the D.T.s— *delirium tremens*—was a hazard of the profession.

The Sergeant told the Lieutenant, "He's got the D.T.s! He thinks he's arrested a kangaroo!"

The Lieutenant immediately made a decision: "We aren't going to make a report, and we're going to take care of that poor man before anyone finds out. We're taking him to Duffy's right away." Duffy's was a dry-out farm for alcoholics up in Sonoma that had a contract with the San Francisco Police Department to rescue those cops who needed to get religion about their drinking.

The Sergeant was in agreement. So the Sergeant and the Lieutenant immediately changed into their civilian clothes, and got into an unmarked car to go up to their poor, hallucinating officer. They drove up to Sixth and Minna.

We all make judgments about other people, even people we like, and those judgments are not based on a full investigation of all the facts, but on those bits of knowledge we may think we have. We do it all the time. Sometimes, we are right. And sometimes, we hurt people because we make judgments on incomplete facts that are wrong.

The Sergeant was driving the car, and he pulled up to the corner of Sixth and Minna. The Lieutenant rolled down the window and said gently to the officer, "It's going to be OK. Get in, we're driving you to Duffy's."

The officer, compliant as always, said, "Sure Lieutenant. But what should I do about the kangaroo?"

And there, handcuffed to a parking meter, was a kangaroo that had escaped from a traveling circus, and which had been enjoying its liberty until it was arrested by the beat man.

Gift of the Magi

When he retired, my friend was the oldest legitimately working policeman I ever knew, 72 years old.

I say "legitimately," because there was one policeman I knew who had been older. One guy had been on the motorcycles until he was 74, or 76, or 77, depending on which birth certificate you believed, back when you had to retire when you were 65. Every so often the retirement board would ask him if he wasn't over retirement age, and he'd have to send back to Ireland for another phony birth certificate. The motorcycle cop was so old he couldn't kick start his Harley, so he just left it running, all day and all night. Guys were putting up fake pictures of him standing next to Lincoln at Gettysburg in his motorcycle helmet. Finally, when the personnel office calculated that even if he had been 21 when he came in, he would still be well over 65, the motorcycle cop retired —and six months later he was dead.

Some people shouldn't ever retire.

But then the mandatory retirement age was abolished, so my friend could work as long as he wanted. And he wanted to work.

Being a policeman is fun, it really is. You deal with danger, and tragedy, and sadness, but it is adventurous, it is interesting, it is exciting, and you spend time with other cops, whom you like. They give you the best toys a kid ever wanted—a badge and a gun, and you get to play cops and robbers with real robbers.

People watch police shows because they are interesting and exciting. But we cops get to live it, and it's twenty times as good as television. It's like the difference between watching the Indianapolis 500, and actually driving a race car. There's no comparison.

Since my friend had qualified for the maximum pension, he was working for about three dollars an hour more than he would get just staying home and collecting on his retirement—but he didn't care. There is always something interesting to do when you're a policeman, something exciting coming your way when you least expect it, someone to meet whom you can happily remember later on.

My friend had the kindest heart of all. I have always been proud to say he is my friend. In fact, he is really more of a brother to me; he was my partner longer than anybody. My friend was kind, generous to a fault, and gentle. They say police are in a brotherhood—and it's true. I felt my friend was my brother.

My friend showed love to everyone he met. If there was anything he could do for you, he would do it.

My friend got a reputation for kindness throughout the Department. Communications learned that if they got a call from a nut, they could get rid of it by transferring it to my friend, who was in Operations Center. For a while I worked there with my friend, so I know.   One woman used to call all the time threatening suicide. Crazy Cathy, we called her. At first, we sent cars out to put a butterfly net over her, but after she was released so many times from the psych ward, we stopped. She took up so much of everybody's time that she was forbidden by Suicide Prevention to call more than once a night. She could kill herself once a day, but no more. But my friend would talk to her. Most other people would hang up on such lunatics, but my friend was nice to everybody. That meant that they would pester him several times a night, but my friend had a sense of duty to needy people.

Another lonely, dingy guy used to call, to tell us that there were whores on Leavenworth Street, and drunks in the Tenderloin bars. He said Army Intelligence had sent him to advise King Hassan of Morocco. He frequently called us from King Hassan's palace. The phone calls from the royal palace were hysterical. The phones in Morocco sounded just like Geary Street phone booths. You could hear the 38 Geary bus going by.

My friend had a conference call with Crazy Cathy and King Hassan's friend one time. They met on the phone, and dated. Cathy later called up and said, "That guy is really crazy."

One fellow used to call, and told us he was Agent 007. He thought of himself as the secret undercover source of information for the police. He would call with the latest crime news: there are people sleeping on the sidewalk outside St. Anthony's homeless shelter. He got in trouble because he heard footsteps coming up the stairs of his apartment building, and he knew it was someone who was trying to get him,, so he spread lighter fluid on his carpet, set fire to it to make a diversion, and jumped out his front window. That earned him a trip to the psych ward. After he got out of the hospital, he started calling again, so my friend told him the LAPD wanted our best agent, and asked him to go. We didn't hear from him again—but we did hear from an LAPD Sergeant who asked if he really was our agent.

My friend worked nights, and in the daytime he cared for his mother, who was very elderly, and very ill. She was wheelchair-bound, and she'd wake him up several times during the day to do things for her. He would come to work exhausted. When she died, my friend was devastated.

My friend had police work to buoy him up, however, and after a while he was his old cheerful self—just not as sleepy.

He was tall and slim, and handsome—even when he retired. He used to date a lot of women—some good-looking women—but he never married them. Somehow, they weren't quite right for him.

But then my friend's sister got sick. She was a regular medical encyclopedia, and the worst thing she had was emphysema—terminal emphysema. My friend insisted on taking her into his home so that he could personally care for her. Once again, he was working nights and caring for someone in the daytime. But this time, he was 72, and that's too old to burn the candle at both ends.

My friend's house became a nursing facility for his sister. Another cop who knew my friend was discussing this with me. He said, "It's as if an angel whispered in his ear, 'If you give your property over to your sibling, you'll go to heaven, for sure.' I know he will be rewarded for that." I had to agree.

He gave his home over to his dying sister, and he did it just because it was the right thing to do. He cared for her, night and day, and for the times he couldn't be with her, he arranged for professional care. You couldn't ask for a better brother than my friend. It must have been hard, but he did it—and he did it cheerfully. I agreed with the other cop—my friend will have a place in heaven.

It came to this: my friend had to quit working for the police, or he had to quit caring for his sister. With great sadness, he retired. It was his gift to his dying sister.

We had a party and a ceremony for him. He was too choked up to say much at either event.

About six weeks after my friend retired, his sister died.

I went to the wake. My friend was standing by the coffin, looking down at his sister.

She was all he had. He had never married. Now he didn't have his mother, and he didn't have his sister, and he had retired from the police.

I walked up to him.

His cheeks were wet with tears.

Gone With The Wind

I met him when we were trying to catch his father. His old man had blasted a neighbor's front door with a shotgun in an attempt to collect a $5 debt, and we thought we could catch him at home. It was almost a military operation: a huge guy from the Tac Squad led the way upstairs with a Garand rifle. I followed with a shotgun, and a couple of men with magnum revolvers were right behind. But his father had slipped out, with the shotgun.

He lived in the projects on top of Hunter's Point hill, an area where shootings were common. His mother was in the living room, swaying back and forth in an old rocking chair, talking loudly to nobody in particular, calling out a free-associating stream of utter nonsense. She did not respond to anybody's questions. We considered taking her to a mental hospital.

"She'll be all right," he said. "She gets this way, but then she snaps out of it."

I talked to him for a while, originally to try to find out where his father might be hiding, but then in amazement. Here was a kid with a drunken criminal for a father and a psychotic for a mother, living in the projects, with nothing of value in his home, and he had ambitions, with a fierce intelligence that made me think that he might succeed.

He went to George Washington High School all the way across the City, which meant that he had to travel two hours on a bus every day, but it was fine with him because he wanted to go to a good school. He was seventeen, and he wanted to be a doctor. He spoke the King's English, which was remarkable because nobody in his family talked that way. His grammar was perfect, and his vocabulary was formidable. A friend of his walked by, and they had a brief conversation in the heavily accented, slang-peppered speech common in the ghetto. When his friend was gone, he instantly switched back to standard English. *This kid knows two languages—perfectly*, I thought.

We discussed his college plans. He wanted to go to Berkeley, and he thought he would get in because his grades were good. After Berkeley, he wanted to go to UCSF Medical School. I looked around his house. There were no books except his high school texts. He was getting straight As with no help at home, nobody to give him advice on his homework, no one who even cared if he even went to class. His family did not have a telephone. He couldn't call up a classmate for advice. Most kids could rely on their parents for help with a term paper or a class project—but not this young man. He had nothing. But all by himself, he was doing just fine.

He was a parent to his mother and father. He took his mother regularly to a mental health clinic, and accompanied his father to AA meetings. None of this discouraged him: he was going to succeed. He knew it, with a knowledge that came from a hot steel will. And after a while, I knew it, too.

I was standing with him on the sidewalk. The project apartments where he lived were covered with scrawled obscenities. Within a block's radius, I had seen two homicides that week: a father had died in my arms with a kitchen knife put through his gut by his own son, and a young gangster had collected a bullet in the neck a few doors down. I myself had been shot at when I drove up Middlepoint Road three weeks earlier.

The desperation of the place was palpable. Nobody had a good job, nobody had an education, nobody had money. No child on the entire hill, I reckoned, had an encyclopedia to help with homework. The most common cause of death for young people was murder. The hopes and lives of the young in that place vanish, as if blown away by the wind that howls up the sides of the hill.

The bones of stolen and stripped automobiles were frequently found on his street. It was not at all remarkable to hear gunshots at any hour of the night.

And in this frightful place, in this vortex of poverty and ignorance, this young man grew up knowing that he would be a doctor. Out of the mud grows the lotus.

I left him feeling somehow elated, as if I had seen a flower, blooming in a desert.

One night a month later I went to his home, just to check up on him. His front door was open. The lights were out, and I couldn't turn them on. The moonlight came through the curtainless windows. I saw that nobody was home. I asked a neighbor what had happened to him, and the neighbor only said that they had moved, but she didn't know where. The only furniture left was the old rocker. There was an open window, and a strong wind came through it, making the rocking chair move back and forth, and causing a cabinet door in the kitchen to slam.

I never saw him again.

Fellini Shoots a Scene on Sixth Street

It was a bad day for a shooting.

One must not conclude that there are good days for a shooting, but there are days that are especially bad, and this was one of them

The reason was that we had worked like dogs in the Iditarod to clean up Sixth Street, and to prevent shootings, and the Mayor Himself was going to come onto Sixth Street to pronounce it safe, and the Captain was hoping against hope that this remarkable turn of events would mean that he would eventually be anointed to a High Position, perhaps even Commander or Deputy Chief. Sixth Street had two thousand reported felonies a year, in a two-block area, and it had been almost two whole months since someone had been murdered; so this miraculous situation warranted a press conference, and proud statements by high officials, and hopes for promotion.

But it was not to be.

The reason that it was not to be was that about an hour and a half before His Honor the Mayor was to hold a press conference at 6th and Stevenson, heart of the crime meltdown in the Southern, a dope dealer neglected to pay his debt.

You must understand that the recommended business practices of dope dealing are not the same as those in the business of, say, trading pork belly futures. Narcotics are illegal, and that means that the remedies that are available to Wall Street investors when they are cheated—as they almost always are—by some serpent in a two-thousand-dollar suit, are unavailable to those who have invested in wholesale cocaine. One may not go to a Land Shark—a lawyer—and ask that the miscreant's ass be hauled into court. Courts are unavailable. Lawyers are unavailable.

The problem is compounded by the fact that to move the inventory of narcotics, one must put the narcotics in the hands of addicts, those whose hunger for the product they are selling is so ferocious that it cannot be described. One must give the dope fiends the dope they crave, so they can sell it instead of use it. And to make that happen, it is necessary to instruct the sales force in the Inexorable Law of Economics as it applies to narcotics: if you don't pay for the dope, you will die.

There is no other way. You are not only putting the mouse in charge of the cheese, you are sending out a sales force of mice to peddle the cheese, and the only way the cheese will be sold and not be consumed is to make it clear that to eat the cheese is death.

The narcotics trade is founded on two things: a need for the dope which is as sharp as a cobra's bite, and a casual violence that is indescribable in its brutality.

On this day, a dope fiend, unable to resist, had smoked the crack he was supposed to sell, and he was unable to pay his debt to the wholesaler, and the wholesaler did what every other right-thinking dope-ring middleman does: he pulled out a .45 pistol, a hand-cannon of enormous power, and chased his offending employee out into the street, where he explained the Golden Parachute and other terms of the termination of employment package by putting two large lead slugs though the employee's rib cage, and, simply due to a lack of practice at the pistol range, two or three other slugs into the wall of the Wendy's restaurant across the street.

The terminated employee breathed his last on the blacktop pavement, about eighty minutes before the Lord Mayor was to pronounce the area safe.

The beat man on whose territory the downsizing occurred was called to the scene, surveyed the cooling corpse of the fired salesman, and with a look of suffering worthy of a cherub in Giotto's *Lamentation*, called for an ambulance, the Coroner, the Crime Lab, Homicide, a Sergeant, and—most painfully of all—the Captain.

The Captain arrived, looking as grief-stricken as if somebody had run over his dog. He was not dressed for the occasion. He was outfitted in his most magnificent dress uniform, his finery pressed and polished and tailored as befits a glorious Captain on the rise, one who can tame even the Sixth Street drug lords, one who is surely headed for higher office. He looked at the blood on the pavement and the pale face of the departed pharmaceutical salesman, and his face assumed a pallor that made the onlookers think that the Captain was headed for Holy Cross Cemetery himself.

A crime lab technician was attempting to get the stray slugs out of Wendy's Restaurant wall, but was having difficulty determining which of the bullet holes in the eatery wall were from this particular shooting.

The Captain stood at attention, his glazed eyes fixedly staring at the corpse.

Police cars blocked the street, so traffic backed up. A junior officer put up yellow "Police Line Do Not Cross" tape across the entire street.

The Coroner arrived, parked his meat wagon at the corner, and sauntered up to his new client, all the time eating a salami sandwich. "He's dead, all right," the Coroner said, and with that, the beat officer breathed a sigh of relief, because he would now be authorized to turn over the case to the Homicide dicks, and that meant that his job was almost over.

Two other cops asked everyone on the sidewalk for witness information. Nobody, of course, could recall having seen or heard anything.

TV photographers showed up, put large cameras on tripods that must have weighed sixty pounds apiece, and started filming.

A tourist came to the intersection of Sixth and Market, and looked at the panorama before him with the joy and glee of St. John viewing the Resurrection. "Look, Ma!" he said to his wife. "They're shooting a movie! I knew we'd see this if we came to California!" They were dressed in shorts, sandals, Hawaiian shirts, cameras about their necks and bouncing on their ample bellies, and straw hats. The tourist stood almost dancing with happiness that he could witness the greatness of the occasion.

The Captain had not moved.

The Photo Lab technician began to take still photographs of the body with a huge camera and a giant flash that illuminated the corpse like a second sun.

The tourist asked the Captain, "What's going on?"

"Shooting," said the Captain, still in shock and fighting the urge to throw up.

"What movie are they shooting?" the tourist persisted.

"Homicide," the Captain whispered from a mouth filled with the ashes of his career.

The tourist looked at the assembled news cameras, and he suddenly realized: this was a major Hollywood event. Somewhere, close by, was a great star. His joy turned to ecstasy. He had wandered from the dentists' convention to this wonderful surprise, the shooting of "Homicide," the next Hollywood blockbuster.

A used-up whore from one of the Sixth Street flophouse hotels approached the strange couple from the Midwest, and smiled, "Looking for excitement?" The tourist looked into her mouth, and saw only her missing incisors. "You'd better have that taken care of," he told her, completely oblivious to her suggestion. He turned his attention back to the vista God had ordained him to witness.

A drunk stumbled from a bar, a large mug of beer in his hand, the sour odor of stale beer and urine following him out onto the street. He looked at the corpse. "Hey, I know him!" he said. "Billy! Sorry it happened to you! Here, have a drink!" And with that, he poured a generous slug of beer onto the corpse.

The Photo Lab technician almost dropped his camera in alarm. Right before him, a drunk was destroying evidence, ruining his crime scene, giving Johnny Cochran the very ammunition he would need to embarrass him in front of the whole world. "My scene! My scene!" he shouted. "You're ruining my scene!"

The tourist looked as if he had seen the Beatific Vision. He had finally been able to see the shooting of a Hollywood scene.

Reincarnation

My friend lived enough adventures for twenty ordinary lives.

In the early 1970s, it was very common for police to be shot at; it was the time of the Vietnam War, and political radicals were encouraging conflict with the police—the "pigs," they called us.

Most cops on patrol on the Midnights carried a carbine in their car; I was an exception. After I got pinned down by a sniper one night, I resolved to have something with me at all times with which I could shoot back at long distances, so I acquired an Artillery Model Luger, the longest pistol I could find.

Another exception was my friend. He didn't carry a rifle—he carried a grenade.

My friend was a unique guy, and he had a lot of adventures, one of which unfortunately involved the grenade.

He was riding with a rookie at about three in the morning, and as they came near City Hall, the rookie said, "Is it true you carry a grenade?"

My friend said it was, and the rookie asked to see it.

My friend handed the grenade to the rookie—and the rookie promptly pulled the pin.

Pulling the pin of a grenade means that you have about five seconds until it explodes.

Fortunately, the window of the car was open. My friend grabbed the grenade, threw it over the top of the police car into the reflecting pool that was in front of City Hall, and stomped on the accelerator. They got a few yards away when the grenade went off with a huge boom. There was thousands of dollars damage to the pool—but the two cops didn't report it, and when we heard of the story, we kept it to ourselves.

My friend was one of the most aggressive cops in the business. He got into a running gunfight with two robbers, and killed both of them under very heroic circumstances. The gun he did it with was a Smith & Wesson .38. The Smith & Wesson Company heard of the gunfight, and had a master gun engraver work the revolver into a beautiful piece of art.

He had quite a sense of humor. For a while, he was in the canine unit, and he had a huge German shepherd in the back of his station wagon. One evening, while he was eating, a tourist came up to him and asked him what kind of a dog it was that was in the back of his patrol car. At this time, the dog was howling like a wolf. My friend said, "That's no dog, that's a California werewolf." The tourist backed away very slowly from the car, and went into a restaurant. He emerged with his wife, and told her, in shocked tones, that this was a California werewolf working for the police. His wife didn't seem any brighter than he was: she took a flash picture of it to show her friends back home.

My friend saw that robbers in the Tenderloin were picking on old people, so he led a decoy squad. My friend regarded himself as the protector of the old and the weak. He dressed up as a poor old man with a cane, and limped down the street. Robbers attacked him, and sometimes hurt him—but then he made the arrest. Altogether, he was robbed more than five hundred times.

I could never understand why anyone would try to rob him, because even though he was not a large man, his eyes had a ferocious glow, an "I'm going to kill you" expression. You just look at some people, and you know they are dangerous; he was one of them. He solved that problem by always looking at the ground when he was in the decoy squad.

My friend's beloved son died, and we all thought that the grief caused him to become a little unhinged.

He was widowed for some years when his son died. After that, he acquired a much younger girlfriend. He took some pictures of her, naked, and showed them to other cops.

It was not unusual for cops to have pictures of naked women inside their lockers, and a lot of guys doubtless had sexy pictures of their wives or girlfriends. But pictures of wives or girlfriends were not shared with other guys, just as the women themselves were not shared with other guys. We all kind of thought this behavior was unusual—almost alarming.

My friend knew more jokes than anyone else I ever knew—and his sense of humor was keenly developed. But underneath the laughter, he was a very sad man. He missed his son. His humor was the attempt of a drowning man to grab a life preserver. We respected him, but we worried about him.

And then he did something else that stirred strong debate among the rest of the cops.

He became a Civil War buff. He collected Civil War memorabilia, and he had two glass display cases in his home with two complete, authentic uniforms—one blue, and one gray.

One night, he told us that he believed he was a reincarnated Civil War officer from J.E.B. Stuart's cavalry.

This stirred considerable controversy.

Most people with any sense know enough not to argue with a cop. And police absolutely will not argue with civilians. Cops just tell you to do something, and if you refuse, the cops will make you do it. But that is not to say that police do not argue among themselves. And those arguments are sometimes on a very high intellectual level.

Some thought he was going nuts, and some thought he might be right. There was a debate as to whether Christianity could be reconciled with reincarnation, and whether scripture talks about it at all; some thought that when Jesus asked the apostles who people were saying he was, and the reply was that some people thought he was Elijah, that meant that there was some belief in reincarnation, even though that is certainly not mainstream Christian or Jewish thought.

Then the debate shifted to the possibility that there are other explanations for instances people cite to support reincarnation.

People think cops operate on a very practical intellectual level, but that isn't entirely true. The police force is like the Army: you have highly educated people working alongside others who were lucky to get out of high school. The discussion about reincarnation was an example of this.

We were standing around the station office, waiting for our shift to begin, discussing the theories of people who thought you get knowledge by tapping into a vast mental library, like a World Soul: Plato, Plotinus, and Jung.

So, we debated whether it is possible to see the future or the past because your mind taps into a World Soul. We debated whether imaginary dragons are images left over from the terror of our pre-human ancestors who were chased by dinosaurs, as Jung seems to imply. Some said that is why people in every culture think of dragons, even cultures which are isolated from others.

And we argued over whether bees know how to make a hive because they tap into the knowledge of God. A Lieutenant asked, "Have you thought about it? Here is a spider, with a brain the size of the head of a pin, and she knows how to use eight legs, and how to spin a web, which is the same web every other spider of her type spins. She knows it, without learning it. We say, 'Well, that's instinct.' Sure, but 'instinct' is a label, not an explanation.

"Plotinus thought there was a 'Nous,' or 'World Soul,' into which we can tap for some knowledge. Plato thought the same."

Everyone was silent after the Lieutenant had stopped speaking—but the silence did not last long.

A Sergeant asked, "Do we get thoughts from God? Isaiah 53 is the proof that we get knowledge from God, directly. Isaiah couldn't possibly have known what he was writing about, hundreds of years before it happened."

The Lieutenant answered: "Plato had a theory of knowledge as recollection. We used to exist before this, and know everything. Now we remember it, sort of, and we perhaps have some communication with what Plotinus would call the Nous."

One Sergeant had the opinion that there is no physical difference between the live body and a dead body, and that the difference that causes life must therefore be nonphysical—a soul. He also said that in thought, there is freedom. And since the soul is not physical, it is not affected by physical death. The body can die, because it is physical, but not the soul.

But another officer said that doesn't prove that souls are pre-existing, and don't go from body to body.

We discussed different incidents that seemed to prove reincarnation.

Then another Sergeant opined that examples of what we take for reincarnation can be explained by the Swiss psychiatrist Carl Jung's theories of the Collective Unconscious and of Archetypes—that the thoughts and experiences of all living things don't just fade away, but are contained in something like a cosmic record that we can mentally access. People all around the world have the same symbols, even in isolated cultures.

The Sergeant said that the Collective Unconscious is like a library of everyone's thoughts. So maybe, if you're remembering past lives, you really are remembering them —but they're not your past lives, there someone else's, and you've just mentally tapped into the cosmic recording of their experiences.

And that is the way that the debate went, back and forth, between policemen. You might expect policemen to debate whether a revolver is better than a semi-automatic pistol, and they do debate that—but you don't expect to walk into a police station and hear an argument over philosophers like Plotinus.

At that point, the station secretary walked in, mouth agape at this discussion. The booking Sergeant gave her a wicked grin and laughed, "And you think all we do is tell fuck stories!"

But my friend never participated in these debates; to him, it was simply the reality of his life that he had been in the Civil War.

Eventually, he decided that he had enough of police work, and he retired.

He wrote a book of his experiences, and got it published. The other cops who knew him bought a number of copies, and we enjoyed reading it.

My friend dropped by the station one time, and told me a joke. It was typical of the jokes he told—always original, and always hysterical:

"OK, there's these two rubes, and they're driving their truck down the street, and they see a gas station. The gas station has a sign that says, 'Free Sex With Gas!' So they pull in, and order a fill-up, and then the driver asks the attendant, 'Well, what about my free sex?' And the attendant says, 'OK, pick a number between one and ten.' And the driver says, 'Three.' The attendant says, 'Sorry, the number is seven.' So the other rube says, 'Can I try?' And the attendant says, 'Sure.' And the other rube says, 'Four.' And the attendant says, 'Sorry, I already said, the number is seven. Try again next time.' So they pull out and go back on the street. And so the passenger says to the driver, 'Do you think that's for real?' And the driver says, 'Oh, yeah, it's for real, all right. My wife was in twice, and she won both times.'"

We talked a little, and I asked him what he planned to do next.

"Oh, I've got a lot of things planned," he said, "Too much for one lifetime, even." He laughed.

A couple of weeks later, he was dead of a heart attack.

Ghost Story

The universe does not always cooperate with our attempts to categorize it. Sometimes, we open a door in our world, and look out onto a frightening, alien landscape that we don't expect. The world we know in daylight is perhaps not the only world we live in. There are intelligences that live in the darkness of the universe, and some of them are not kind.

Police are not equipped to patrol other worlds, but sometimes we encounter them.

In the early 1970s, such a demonic encounter was whispered about among policemen. We were confronted with a growling, snarling experience of otherness, and we didn't like it, not at all.

On a tiny street called Vega, not far from the old Sears store at Masonic and Geary, was a grammar school. It is presently called Wallenberg Alternative High School, but it had previous names when it was a grammar school. The local residents never call it by its proper name, however: it was always just called "the school that Khrushchev visited," because when the Soviet premier visited San Francisco, he walked through that school.

About a dozen years after the visit by Khrushchev, another, darker incident happened at that school, and the police spoke to each other about it—at first quietly, so that no one would think they were odd, and then openly, but in tones of terrified awe.

I learned the details from one of the officers who had been called to the school. I was working as a Cadet in the Planning and Research Bureau, and a tall, handsome, dark-haired officer came in to get some of our publications. One of the cops who worked with me said to us, "That's him, he's one of the guys who went to the school that Khrushchev visited!" And we all surrounded him. After much cajoling, and assurances that we would take him seriously, he finally told us his chilling story.

A teacher from the school, much beloved by her pupils, had gone to Africa during summer vacation. She was reputed to be interested in the native religions of Africa, and she had studied extensively about shamanism, mysticism, black magic, and demonic pagan beliefs. She had wanted to meet some witch doctors, and to study their practices. Some of her fellow teachers thought her interest in the black arts had turned from the academic to the practical.

But when the new fall semester started, she was nowhere to be found. She didn't come to school, and she hadn't returned home. Her family hadn't heard from her, and was rapidly getting frantic. The State Department promised to help, but it came up with no information. As days turned into weeks, with no communication from her, the family went to the expense of hiring a private investigator.

In gloomy October, in the after-school dusk, several children were playing in the cold, windswept school yard, when they heard a tapping at a classroom window. They turned to look—and behind the glass stood the missing teacher. They rushed into the school, but the classroom door was locked.

The children ran to the principal, who tried to open the door—but the door was locked from the inside, and the school custodian was called in to break it open with his tools.

No one was in the classroom.

The principal called the police, to report that the teacher was seen on campus.

The cops arrived, and talked to the frightened children and the perplexed principal, but they were unable to find the teacher. The classroom seemed unnaturally cold, even colder than the October wind howling in from the deep sea, and no one could explain how the door came to be locked from the inside. The police made a "suspicious occurrence" report, just to document what people told them. And that was all they could do.

But it was not the end of the matter. The frightful experiences of that October were just beginning.

The investigator that the missing teacher's family hired reported back from Africa, and the news was grim. The teacher was dead.

Further news, as it filtered back from the Dark Continent, was even more alarming, and given the circumstances of the dead teacher being seen in her classroom window by several students, people began to become frightened.

The dead teacher's body had been given an autopsy by a local doctor, who had said that her heart had been torn apart from the inside.

The investigator also reported that before she died, the teacher had become involved in a dispute with a witch doctor. What horror awaited her deep in Africa we never learned, except that she did not survive it.

A few days later, again in the gathering gloom of late afternoon, several students once again saw the teacher in her classroom window, and once again, the police were called. The classroom was empty, just as before, although this time, the lock on the door which had been previously removed by the janitor had not been replaced, so entry into the cavernous classroom was not difficult.

This time, a student took one of the policemen aside and told him that the janitor, a deeply religious man, had told the student that he was asked to unclog a drain in a washbasin in the classroom. He could not unclog the drain. He looked under the basin, and saw a small crucifix tied to the drainpipe. When the janitor removed the crucifix, the student said, the water drained from the basin.

The police asked to speak to the custodian, but he refused to say anything, and merely gave them frightened looks when they inquired about the student's story.

The officer's account sparked an intense discussion among the police who surrounded him, a debate that raised the hairs on my neck.

A sergeant ventured the opinion that some pagan sorcerers, such as African and Haitian witch doctors, Indian medicine men, and Hawaiian Kahunas, can summon occult powers that can control or even kill people from a distance. "There are spirits that are more dangerous than any wild animal," he said. "You are better off diving in with a shark in your swimming pool."

An officer offered the opinion that such things depend on the power of suggestion, and you have to believe in their powers before they can affect you.

Another officer disagreed, and said that the universe is like a mansion with many rooms, and we are in one of them, but other, elder, inhuman powers are in rooms near ours, and they keep trying to get in; if we open the door, we can let them in. He said, "Summoning the devil is the easy part. That's no trick at all. The hard part is getting rid of him."

Another cop agreed: "There is evil in the universe," he said, "And if you play with it, you come under its power."

We all wondered whether this was real. But there was no doubt about how the cop who had been there felt about it: he believed it, and he didn't like it at all. He said, "I'm never going back to that school. I don't care what happens, I'm not setting foot there. There's something about that place that gives me the creeps."

Ashes to Ashes, Dust to Dust

It was a warm midsummer's day on skid row, and it was getting warmer. I hadn't eaten anything since the previous evening, so I stopped for a couple of slices of pizza.

There are only two restaurants where I would dare eat on Sixth Street. One is a vegetarian Hindu joint where they are so fanatic about cleanliness they won't even shake hands with you, and the other is a pizza parlor I watched them build in the old Rose Hotel. Every other place is so filthy I wouldn't eat there if I had just been let out of a concentration camp.

I sat in a counter by a window to munch my pizza when a dried-up whore came by, and looked through the window at my pizza with such sorrow and hunger that I held up a piece to offer it to her. She nodded happily, and I took it out to her on a paper napkin. She was probably about forty, but she looked seventy. Dope does that to you.

Her delight was palpable. "Gee, thanks, Officer," she said. She smiled broadly, revealing a mouth with most of its teeth gone.

"Enjoy," I said.

"Hey, thanks! Here's for you! Look at this!" she said, and opened her shirt to reveal shriveled nipples hanging down like the statue of the Mother Wolf who suckled the Founders of Rome: I expected Romulus and Remus to come skipping by any minute. She was thanking me the only way she knew how: after a lifetime of selling her body, her thanks were always physical. Like all the other psychotics in the area, there was no explaining to her that she should act otherwise. And now she was hungry: by the time a whore lands on Sixth Street, she doesn't have anything left to sell that anyone wants to buy.

I sighed, "That's not necessary. Just put your clothes on, and here's the pizza." She took the pizza, one wolf tit still hanging out of her shirt, and danced off eating it. I heard her joyously tell a passerby, "Look what the policeman gave me!" I went back to the pizza parlor to finish my meal, but my appetite was a little shot.

As I finished, we got a call of an 802, a dead person, in a flophouse hotel near Mission Street.

I wasn't far away, but by the time I got there, two beat men were already on the scene.

The owner of the flophouse hotel led us up creaking wooden stairs and narrow corridors. Dope addicts, used-up prostitutes, and impoverished alcoholic pensioners were the main tenants, because nobody with any money would want to live in such a place. The summer heat, the dark, narrow corridors, and the smells of curry made our journey a challenge to our churning stomachs. But we knew a greater challenge awaited.

I walked up three flights of stairs, past the smells of urine from the rooms of the tenants, and curry cooking in the manager's apartments. We got to the door of the room. It was locked.

The manager, an East Indian, said that he hadn't heard from the tenant in a week, and his rent was due. That last, of course, was the real reason for the manager's concern. The hotel owner knocked on the door. There was no response. The smell wafting through the doorjamb announced that the tenant had met his end.

There are three main ways police determined that the occupant of any home is dead: they pound on the door and receive no response; they see flies on a window; and there is a smell. There was no window leading into the corridor, but we could smell the distinctive stench of rotting flesh when we approached the door.

We hated these calls. The powerful aroma of a rotted corpse stays in your nose and your clothes. It ruins your meals for ages, and you can't get rid of it.

Some cops carry gas masks in their patrol car trunks for such occasions, but that isn't an option for cops on the foot beat, and I believed in walking a foot beat as the most effective way to stop crime. I was on foot that day.

A homicide dick told me he carried a cigar to smoke at death scenes. But tobacco makes me sick, and smoking an El Stinko stogie in a room full of choking aromas from a dead body would be like getting punched in the stomach and in the throat at the same time.

So we took one last big gulp of curried air, knowing it would soon seem as fresh as a pine forest. Steeling ourselves not to vomit at the stench, we had the hotel owner open the door. The foul air in the room rolled over us like a hot, suffocating blanket.

We entered to find a man, apparently in his mid-fifties, sitting in a chair. His eyes were open, and he was looking out a window onto Sixth Street. He was dead.

The room was tiny, only about twelve feet long and ten feet wide. The only furniture was the wooden chair the corpse was sitting on, and a badly stained mattress on the floor. There was a blanket crumbled on the mattress. There was no bed frame, no sink, no toilet, no sheets, and no pillows. A small pile of clothes sat neatly folded in the corner. Flies buzzed at the window. The owner had only the tenant's name, and the fact that he had last lived in Modesto. We check our computers, but could find no one from Modesto by that name.

A calendar was tacked onto the wall, a painted Christmas scene hanging cheerily, announcing that it was a December that was five years out of date.

We could find no identification, nor any way of determining who he was, or where he came from.

I looked at his face. I thought, almost in a prayer, *Who are you? Where are you from? How did you come to this wretched place to die? Why do you have no family to care for you?*

I wondered then, as I have often wondered since, why he had no family and no friends to care for him. Did he lead such a lonely life that he had no one that he loved, and no one who loved him?

Love is life: if you don't love, you might still be breathing, but you're already dead.

I thought, *Why does no one care that you are here? Why are you so isolated?*

But like Hamlet asking his questions of poor Yorick's skull, I received no answer.

The coroner's deputies arrived, resplendent in uniforms that made them look like airline pilots. *The Valkyries are coming to take you for a ride,* I thought. I left the officers and the coroner's deputies in charge of the scene, and walked downstairs, breathing deeply of the sickly sweet curried atmosphere.

It was disturbing in a way I could not quite articulate, even though I had been to such incidents many times before. How fragile is our life, that we can be reduced to such loneliness, and then to a corpse, and the only way anyone discovers that we have crossed the Divide is that they are upset that we have failed to pay our rent.

In a hundred years or so, we will all be dead and forgotten. A little over a century ago, my grandfather was a little boy herding geese on a little island, and my other grandfather was in the care of some very kindly nuns in an orphanage. Who remembers them now? In a few years, no one will even know they existed.

If our life's work is to have significance, it must be in the ephemeral moment, in the *now*, not in the way people think of us in years to come. I hope that God observes and remembers the good we do, just as I hope He forgets the bad we perpetrate. That good deed, done in a moment and forgotten in a moment, is all we have. The effects of our deeds are unknowable, like the waves we create when we throw a stone into a pond. We do not know the result of our deeds, or of our lives. We have only the present. In a few years, we will all be ashes and dust, just as in God's curse of Adam.

We do not wish to die; we do not wish to return to dust. But it must be so.

I walked out to Sixth Street, past the coroner's meat wagon, finally smelling the fresh air.

The shriveled whore to whom I had given the pizza walked by, smiled a toothless grin, and said, "Hey, Officer, you're looking down. I hope you're OK! You're sweet." She winked at me. I guess my downcast expression was obvious to everyone.

"Thank you," I said, trying to smile.

I looked up at the hotel window. The dead man was still in his chair, looking down at me.

Black Widow

At 19th and Sloat is a small urban forest called the Sigmund Stern Grove. It is a forest of several blocks' area, composed mainly of eucalyptus and pine trees. You enter at the corner of 19th and Sloat, and go down a steep path into a valley darkened by the thick growth of tall trees on every side. Even in the daylight, it is dark.

Sigmund Stern Grove gives me the creeps even in the daytime, and at night, it is just eerie.

We police try to keep evildoers out of the Grove, so we patrol it frequently.

One midnight, with a full moon overhead, we went down the dark, steep road, and I saw a light. At the bottom of the valley, under an arbor of trees, was a wooden picnic table. Three people were sitting at the table—two men in their early twenties, and a woman of about 35.

On the table, the woman had drawn a pentagram in chalk, and in the center of the pentagram was a lighted candle.

You never know, when you start your shift, what adventures await. It is impossible to predict what calls you will receive, what new troubles you will see. Police work is always interesting, always new, always a surprise.

On several days of the year—Walpurgis Night, the solstices, the equinoxes, the nights of the full moon and the new moon—witchcraft, devil worship, and similar practices are common. They are religious activities protected under the First Amendment, but we keep an eye on them in case they get out of hand.

For instance, one time, we found a headless corpse near Golden Gate Park's panhandle, with feathers stuck in its severed neck, in some kind of voodoo ceremony.

We never did find the head.

We got ID from the three at the table, and ran a records check on them. To our surprise, the two men came back clear—they had no record of any offense. To our further surprise, the woman had a conviction—for homicide.

She was a mousy-looking dame, with dark brown, stringy hair, about 5 foot 6, and very thin. Chronologically, she was in her mid-thirties, but she looked ten years older. There was nothing about her to make you think that she was either a murderer, a witch, or a sexual predator—but she was in fact all three.

She had killed a man during sex, by strangling him. She said it was accidental; some people think that being strangled almost to the point of unconsciousness enhances an orgasm. I am unable to verify that claim. There are certain aspects of sexuality on which I will always have a lack of direct knowledge, and this is one. This strangulation practice has unintentionally resulted in a number of deaths, and this witch's lover was one. She was convicted of the homicide charge, and had only recently been released from prison.

I look at her with astonishment. You would never even notice her if she were passing you by on the street.

We took the two young men aside and told them the situation. They hadn't known the witch had killed someone during sex. The disturbing thing was that they were plainly delighted to hear it.

These two guys were not bright boys.

Normally, I try to stay out of other people's private affairs is much as I can. But in this instance, I felt called upon to try to intervene.

"Do you realize what this means?" I asked.

"Yeah," they said, with wicked smiles.

"Hey, look, guys. Try to think for a minute. This woman already has you worshiping the devil. And she has already killed one man during sex. What do you think is going to happen next?"

"It's going to be fun," one of them said.

I searched for the right words: "Sex *should* be fun. Sex should be loving. Sex shouldn't hurt. Sex shouldn't kill you. This woman is going to *hurt* you. Do you understand that? You can do better than this woman. Why don't you come on out of this place with me? I'll drive you home."

They gave me a look like I was out of my mind. "No, we want to stay with her."

In our psyches, there is a part that represents our opposite. We are attracted to it, and repulsed at the same time. Men may have, for instance, a feminine aspect which psychologists call the *anima*, and which may be further characterized as a positive *anima*, like the Madonna or our mothers, or a dark, negative *anima*, symbolized by a witch or a female vampire. These symbols of women can haunt our unconscious and our dreams, and we may be attracted to real women who correspond to one or another of these symbols, depending on what aspects are important to our developing psyches at that moment.

These men were clearly attracted to this evil woman, but I doubt they could articulate why. They were flies caught in her web.

"No good will come of this," I said. "Why don't you come with me?"

"No, we'll stay," they said. We let them go, as they did their best to wrap themselves in this woman's web.

This rough beast of a woman, her hour come round at last, slouched over her altar table and flashed me a demonic smile of victory and evil anticipation.

We left, and drove silently up the steep path, through the dark overhanging trees, into the street, where we could at last see the stars in the open sky.

Jack

The earliest memory I have of a police officer was of being rescued by one in Golden Gate Park; I guess I was about three. I was being wheeled in a stroller by my mother.

We lived on Fulton Street, across from Golden Gate Park, and a path led practically straight from our house to the Portals of the Past. When San Francisco was destroyed in the 1906 Earthquake and Fire, a prominent mansion was destroyed, except for its Italian marble portico. The entrance was taken to Golden Gate Park and placed by Lloyd Lake, where it was renamed the "Portals of the Past" with a plaque commemorating the disaster for the edification of people strolling by.

My mother took me to feed the ducks at Lloyd Lake, and on this particular afternoon, a man approached us. I don't remember what was wrong, but my mother began screaming for help, and pushed the baby stroller along at a full run. I was quite frightened, but, of course, there was nothing a three-year-old could do. Instantly, a policeman, like a blue, avenging angel, came running along the path, and the man who was following my mother ran off the path into the bushes by the Portals of the Past. The policeman was in full pursuit.

Years later, I had the honor of meeting that policeman, when I also was working for the police. His name was very Russian, and I'll call him Jack. That wasn't his name, but I don't want to use his name without permission. I admired him greatly

When a man has a name like he did, it says something—not so much about him, as it does about his parents. People want to meld into American society, and at the same time retain some individuality. Apple Computer used that desire a few years ago in their advertising slogan, "Fit in. Stand out." You cannot, of course, do both.

His father was a Russian Orthodox priest, who named him after a great Russian hero. None of those "Bill" or "Joe" me-too names for *his* son. And that is the way Ivan grew up. He was his own man.

I grew up in San Francisco's Richmond District. 50,000 Russian immigrants were my neighbors. You could stand on the street corner at 20th and Geary for half an hour, and never hear a word of English spoken.

Nothing Russian is alien to me. They are a warm, loyal people. Most of the people I knew were in the aristocracy who had left Russia after the 1917 Revolution.

When you entered their homes, the first thing you ever saw was a picture of the Czar and his family, framed in black, as if they died yesterday.

We'd have some of them to our home, and it was usually wasn't long before they fell to plotting a counter-revolution. They were deadly serious about it, too. Some of our friends were big leaders in anti-Soviet propaganda, and to me, as a little kid, it was thrilling to hear revolution being plotted in my own home. Some people thought they were crazy to even try it, but of course, as things turned out, they weren't quite so crazy after all.

The Russian culture is both sweet and sad, like life. The Russians do not flinch from a sharp observation of the evil of the world, and they take heroic, unselfish steps to stop it. It was lunacy for Napoleon or Hitler to imagine that they could conquer such a people.

If you give them a chance, they will love you. I have entered the homes of old Russian royalty, and you would have thought, from the reception I got, that I was the Czar himself, raised from the dead. They might not have anything in their cupboard but tea and cookies, but nothing will do if you entered their homes but that you must sit in a comfortable chair while they drag out their ancient China for cookies and tea from a big silver samovar.

Russian life centered around church, which was very important, both in their history, and in their efforts to overthrow communism.

The Russians converted to Christianity in the 10th Century when the prince of Kiev determined that they should have a state religion. He appointed a committee to determine what religion they should have. The committee went to Arabia and Greece, and then returned. They said, "The big advantage of Islam is that you get to have four wives, but the Greek Orthodox ceremonies are so beautiful that we have to become Christians." And so it was.

They traded three wives for ceremony, and as beautiful as some of those Russian women are, it still turned out that they did not lose out on the deal.

Russian Orthodox and Russian Catholic ceremony is even more beautiful than the Greek Orthodox, which is itself so stunning that it is other-worldly. There cannot be a more beautiful service in the universe. Ceremony expresses things that cannot be expressed in words, and communicates things that are otherwise incommunicable. This changes you. It gets you in touch with your spiritual side, and your unconscious. It is nothing for these people to go on for two or three hours in their worship, which has a rhythm and tone that is hypnotic. You feel elevated—almost transported. It is a mystical experience.

It was from this culture that Ivan came.

I ran into him about seventeen years after he had saved me and my mother. I was a Police Cadet, working in the evidence room, and he was a detective. He would come in, examine evidence, and we would discuss cases, gossip in the Department, where you could get the best *piroshki*, Shakespeare—a thousand things. He dealt with life in a gently humorous way. He had to fill out a form to release property to its owner, and the papers called for a listing of "the property, to wit:"—and he said, "Well, you're the only wit around here, so maybe I should put your name down." But that wasn't true. He was also a wit.

Other cops, intimidated by the pronunciation of his real name, just called him by a shortened version; I'll just use "Jack."

A few years after I became a full-fledged police officer, I went to an FBI school with him.

The FBI school was in hostage negotiation. When D. B. Cooper hijacked a plane and got a couple of hundred thousand dollars out of the FBI, the FBI decided to sponsor a hostage negotiation team on the West Coast, and both Jack and I were selected to be in it.

The presentation by the FBI was always well-planned and professional, because they always wanted everyone to think that they were the premier law-enforcement agency in the United States. "These guys are full of themselves," Jack said to me during a break. "Watch out for them." He was right about that.

They told us some of the details of the D. B. Cooper hijacking which they hadn't told the public. They had always claimed that D. B. Cooper died on the way down when he parachuted out of the plane, but they never said publicly why they knew that. D. B. Cooper had demanded not only the money, but two parachutes—one for himself, and one for a crew member that he was going to kidnap and force to jump with him. As it turned out, he was fortunately the only one who jumped.

The reason why the FBI was so certain that he'd died on the way down was because they gave him two parachutes that wouldn't open. Old J. Edgar Hoover may have worn black lace underpanties, but under those, he had balls of steel. It didn't matter to him that he would be killing an innocent crew member; he would be damned if he would let D. B. Cooper get away with it.

D. B. Cooper thought that by saying he would force an innocent crew member to jump with him, he would ensure that the FBI would give him two good parachutes. He thought wrong.

The FBI wanted to keep that detail private. Jack was not impressed with them. "We Russians have a lot of experience with people like J. Edgar Hoover," he said to me as we ate our humble bag lunches in the garden of the building where the training took place. "He was willing to murder a crew member just make sure that D. B. Cooper didn't get away." And of course, he was right about that, too. "These guys are dangerous. Don't let them suck you into their way of doing things, and don't join them. They'll kill you if you get in their way."

With typical Russian sadness, he did not flinch from the reality. He just went on eating his lunch.

Eventually, Jack retired. He was a friend, and I admired him.

Dos vidanya, Jack.

A Woman Scorned

She was a police dispatcher, working in the radio room. She was a blonde, good-looking, and she had beautiful, porcelain skin.

Some women look great even without makeup, and she was one of them. People who look at houses for sale might think that new wall-to-wall carpets are just there to hide something, and women who wear a lot of makeup signal that underneath all that war paint, they might not look like such a goddess. So she went without much makeup at all. She was truly beautiful.

She fell in love with a policeman—a short, ugly man with a bulbous nose and a mottled complexion. He was a nice enough guy, but none of us could figure out why she decided on him.

We figured he had won the lottery.

But whatever you have, you want something else, something more.

The problem with happiness is that it's all in your head. That is also the solution to the problem about happiness.

We like to think that happiness comes from something outside of us. If we had more money, or this car, or that house, or another job, or a better spouse, or if we were famous, or better looking, then we would be happy.

But it doesn't happen that way. That's why so many Hollywood stars are so miserable.

Happiness comes from the tales we tell ourselves.

We constantly tell ourselves tales. All day long, we say to ourselves that we are happy, or sad, or that things are good, or bad, or that events will turn out right, or tragically. The reason we keep doing the same things repeatedly, is that we keep telling ourselves the same tales. What is going on in your life, on the outside, your environment, your social situation, your job, is affected by what is going on inside your head. If we want to change what our life is like, we need to change our thoughts.

He was unhappy. He decided to change things outside of himself, rather than things inside himself, because he was not a bright man, and he had no idea at all what was going on within his skull. Dull people are often dull because they do not look inside their own souls. That is one reason why you can be both intelligent and dull at the same time.

He met two lesbian police officers, and got to know them pretty well.

There were a lot of theories about why what happened next took place. Freud says that the hidden intention of an action may be found in the result; perhaps, he was having trouble with his wife, and wanted a divorce. Whatever the reason, the two lesbians decided that a little sexual adventure with a man wouldn't be out of the question, and the policeman was happy to oblige.

So, the policeman got into a *ménage a trois* with the two lesbian cops. That was his first mistake. It is possible to stay out of trouble if you are either good, or at least smart. He was neither. He followed his first error with at least two more.

His second mistake was to videotape himself dancing the Devil's Polka with those two women.

And his third mistake was to leave the incriminating videotape in the VCR on his home TV when he went to work. But to refer to Freud again, perhaps this was not a mistake at all, but an unconscious decision that he and the blonde were over.

When his wife came home from her job, she saw the tape in the VCR, and turned it on. There, through the magic of television, was her husband, doing unspeakable things with two women.

Police dispatchers, like police themselves, are trained to handle a crisis calmly and deliberately. She was a good dispatcher, and handled all sorts of crises with an icy calm—including this one.

She told no one what she had seen, and when her husband came home, she had dinner waiting. She gave no indication that she knew anything at all.

Instead, when her husband was next at work, she made a couple of dozen copies of the videotape, and mailed them to all of her husband's friends in the Department. Then she cleaned out their bank accounts, filed for divorce, quit her job, and moved out of the city.

We love to see the ruin of other people, especially people who are more beautiful, or richer, or more famous than we are. We are jealous, and enjoy their destruction.

Hollywood stars have given us such jealous joy for years. But anyone else's destruction will do, and so it took less than a day for everyone in the Department to know what happened.

He couldn't go into any room in police headquarters without people spontaneously bursting into laughter at him.

The two lesbian cops quit the Department. They couldn't stand being humiliated every day by people whispering and laughing about them.

Everyone in the universe makes mistakes. Everyone has done things that seemed like a good idea at the time, but when you think about them later, you wish that you had a rewind button on the VCR of life. But life doesn't come with a rewind button, and what is done, is done.

However, what is done can also be forgiven, and forgotten. His wife didn't forgive him, but other people eventually forgot.

He didn't quit. I don't know whether that was because he had the courage to face up to his difficulties, or because he just didn't see that he had any options. He endured several years of ridicule, and eventually, so many other people had gotten themselves into new kinds of trouble that people's attention was distracted. People got used to having him around. And eventually, most people had forgotten that it even happened.

He put in a lot of effort into his job, and people came to respect him for it, at first grudgingly, and finally without reservation.

He had at last lived it down.

Confession

He was a police Sergeant; and long ago he had made a mistake. He wanted to confess.

Mistakes. We all make mistakes. The world groans under the awful weight of mistakes.

We all do things that seem like a good idea at the time, but later on, they dissolve our peace of mind, like acid.

Children have no concept of this. Children have never done something horribly wrong, nor have they often done anything that was just ill-advised but had terrible consequences flow from it.

Sometimes, the guilt of such a thing is like a hideous cancer in your soul that eats away at you, and it grows and grows until it infects all of your being.

You want to get rid of it, to burn it out, to wipe it off you.

A horrid deed and the inner turmoil it brings constitute an awful secret that separates you from other people. Suddenly, you are alone, miserably isolated from anyone who might love or care about you, and you dare not tell anyone, because you know they will forever shrink from your presence as if you had a contagious disease.

You think that not many people have a secret like that?

You're wrong. Dead wrong. Millions of people have a secret like that.

How many times have you seen naïve friends and family press an Army veteran returning home from war, for stories of combat? And how many times have you seen the veteran blanch and beg off?

Combat veterans often don't want to talk about their experiences. Killing people is a nasty, traumatic business, and it gets even worse for some of these guys because sometimes the people they killed weren't even enemy soldiers. In war, you aren't always sure what you are shooting at. Sometimes they were civilians, or children; sometimes they were even fellow soldiers.

The memory of such deeds remains bottled up inside, like a poison that brings death to all of your organs, slowly, one after the other. It ruins your life. These memories, and the guilt they exact, haunts them like a vampire that sucks the life force out of them forever.

Soldiers aren't the only victims of such guilt.

Lots of other people have painful secrets.

Religions sometimes have ceremonies to get rid of guilt. Jews used to put their sins onto a goat and drive it out into the desert. Now, there is Yom Kippur. Christians have confession, which is really powerful psychic medicine. It is if you magically found the erase button on the VCR of life, so that you could just get rid of your mistakes.

But the Sergeant wasn't confessing to a priest. He confessed to me. I suppose that telling someone about his secret made him feel close to another human being, and drew out the lonely poison that separated him from the rest of humanity.

The Sergeant and I were riding in a patrol car, and we passed a particular intersection.

"I made an arrest, right here, once," he said.

Cops talk to each other about their experiences the way veterans talk to each other. Nobody else would really understand.

He went on: "We drove by, and this guy was standing in the street, naked except for army boots. He had just walked out of one of the gay sex clubs around here, where everybody goes naked into a pitch black dark room, and everybody has sex with everybody else, and they never know who it is they're doing it with.

"So this guy was drunk, and naked except for the boots, and he was covered with grease. And did he ever stink!"

I thought that was going to be the end of the story, but it wasn't.

The Sergeant gave a deep sigh and continued: "I had him in the back of my radio car, and I was angry that he was stinking it up. I told him, 'You peace of shit, why don't you just kill yourself and do the world a favor?'" The Sergeant said this with a voice that started to break.

A hideous thought occurred to me as to where this story was leading, but I didn't interrupt.

Our idea of sexuality is strongly bound up with our idea of what it means to be human.

Witnesses to a crime lots of times cannot tell you how tall a suspect is, or what race, or what they were wearing—but they almost always know whether the suspect was a man or woman.

When we unconsciously refer to someone as sexually neutral, calling them, "it," we are almost ready to kill them. Babies are the only common exception to that rule. Being a full human being means having a sexual identity, and we become profoundly disturbed at people who do not conform to our ideas of male and female roles. We tend to mentally write them off as being not quite human beings.

The Sergeant had done exactly that to his prisoner, and he even told the prisoner that he should die. He thought that man's sexual conduct was so disgusting that he wasn't even human, and that he deserved to die.

The Sergeant slowly whispered, "So I booked him into the jail cell in the station, and when I checked on him again half an hour later, he was dead. He had hanged himself with his boot laces."

Sometimes we think of other people as less than human. The consequences of that are grim.

The Sergeant began to weep.

"God forgive me," he said.

Murphy Man

He was a Murphy Man, which means that he was pimp who does not have a prostitute, but who collects money from customers who think he does have prostitutes working for him.

This particular kind of fraud can get very dangerous for the Murphy Man. But he was a man of steel nerves, and an unerring understanding of the darker needs of the human soul.

Police get a little bit bored running after brainless purse snatchers, and it really is nice once in a while to have to deal with a crook who has some skill. In a perverse way, we enjoyed having him around.

People are under the false impression that the bigger the crime, the more attention it will get from police. But that is absolutely false.

Police pay absolutely no attention at all to the biggest criminals in our society. Police are simply not equipped to handle the things they do, and if they do try to go after the biggest criminals, they are promptly told by their superiors to mind their own business.

The most powerful criminals in the United States are either in politics or in business.

Take politics for instance. The government is an organization that can tax everybody in the country. It doesn't matter how you feel about it, the government can take your property from you. This is a criminal's dream.

But the government doesn't take money from you and give it to crooked people in such a way that you can normally make any real objection. Usually, it is under the guise of a government contract.

For instance, we used to have a huge Main Library in San Francisco. Contractors wanted to build a new Main Library, and make millions of dollars. There was a huge campaign based on the fact that the old Main Library was getting so old that it was liable to fall over in an earthquake, crushing all the library patrons. Clearly, we couldn't have such a situation, and so a bond measure was passed to build a beautiful new Main Library a block away. Many millions of dollars were flushed down the drain, and most of the books were transported from the old Library to the new Library. But the new Library didn't have enough shelf space for *all* the books, so a third of them were taken out of state and dumped in a public landfill. They weren't sold off or given to other libraries in order to prevent the public from knowing that this had gone on. It got out anyway, and there was public outrage.

But then the question was, what do we do with the old Main Library? It was converted into a new Asian Art Museum. I guess that art patrons can be crushed by a falling-over building, and nobody cares—or else, the building wasn't in such bad shape as everybody pretended. They made some seismic repairs, and let the museum patrons back in.

The exact same thing happened in another town I know. The Library was going to be destroyed in an earthquake, money was raised to build a new Library, and once the new Library was finished, the old building was converted into a museum. Contractors got rich, and made big contributions to the politicians who pulled the strings.

This goes on in government every single day. The politicians are not necessarily paid off directly; their friends are paid, and their friends filter the money to them. Or they get "campaign contributions" and have their wives work for the campaign for a salary. Or they have a business on the side, like a law practice, and get huge money from the people who want to buy their influence.

If government is evil, Wall Street is Satanic.

Human serpents walking up and down Wall Street in $2000 Armani suits are very highly respected in the world. It just goes to show that we think that if you have a lot of money, you must be a good person.

These people are the worst crooks of all. These reptiles steal your pension. An ordinary street robber only takes your watch and wallet.

The CEO of a corporation who is paid according to the price of the stock, will frequently stop at nothing to defraud investors if it keeps the stock price high. They can do lots of things that push the stock price up for a moment, but which will ultimately damage the company. Anyone can get the bottom line up in a vehicle fleet: just stop changing the oil. The bottom line goes up, profits are up, the CEO gets millions and quits with a golden parachute, and the next CEO has to deal with a fleet of cars with ruined engines. Sometimes, as in the Enron scandal, everything collapses, and people who have saved all their lives for retirement find that they will be eating dog food anyway. Stock market frauds and corporate mismanagement rob you of your pension, make no mistake about it.

Having your savings tied up in stock out there is like having a rattlesnake somewhere in your bedroom: you might not be getting bitten right now, but the threat is always there, and you want to be able to sleep a little better. Old-time kings used to have a servant whose job it was to jump up and down on their beds to make sure there wasn't a viper under the sheets. We rely on the SEC to do this, but it can only do a tiny bit of what it would need to do in order to really protect us.

And don't think you are protected by your broker. Brokers really only have two things they say about a stock: buy it, or sell it. They're in the business of buying or selling, not holding stock. They don't make money when you hold a stock. Anything analysts say other than "buy" or "strong buy" is translated by knowledgeable people into, "Sell this stock; it's going to tank." "Sell" is the equivalent of a doctor saying a patient is "extremely critical." By the time a hospital says you're "guarded," or "serious," let alone "critical," "extremely critical" or "grave," you are in a very sorry state of disrepair and should always eat dessert first, because you might not have time to get around to it otherwise. Hospitals normally do not say something so understandable as, "Hey, this guy is dying, and there is nothing we can do," unless you have one foot in the grave and the other on a banana peel, and you have already run out of insurance coverage.

So it is with stockbrokers. "Accumulate" means, "Sell, but the company probably isn't filing the bankruptcy papers until tomorrow afternoon, so you might still be able to find a buyer in the morning." "Hold" is equivalent to a polite "sell." Analysts don't really mean hold it. They mean sell it, but for some reason they can't scream out, "Sell, you fools, before you are ruined! If you keep this stock, you'll all be jumping out of windows tomorrow!"

Maybe they can't say it because the company with the bad stock has financial ties to the analyst's company, or the analyst's boss is related to the President of the company with the worthless stock, or for some other reason. Sometimes, I suspect straight bribery. They use polite weasel words to avoid offending people who might still have a financial hold on them.

By the time a securities analyst working for any securities firm finally says, "Sell," the stock is practically dead. You have to translate what people say, sometimes, because they use euphemisms when they don't want to offend people.

When the markets stepped off a cliff between March 2000 and March 2001, and the NASDAQ lost 60% of its value and the Dow 20%, a survey of stock analysts showed a "sell" rating on about 11 of 850 stocks. So, you lose your pension money and eat dog food in your old age.

The biggest frauds are usually in business and the stock market.

But people don't want to believe it. I'll give you an example.

Charles Ponzi is the only person in human history to lend his name to a particular kind of fraud. His name comes up in case law, and even in statutes: "This is a Ponzi scheme!"

Around 1920, Ponzi made it known to a certain lucky few that he could make them money: he, through miraculous investing, would give them a return of 50% within 45 days. A few people invested with Ponzi, and indeed, the checks began rolling in. They received their money, as promised, and they enthusiastically told their friends, who told their friends, and so on. Ponzi brought in nearly ten million dollars before he went to jail, which was a very considerable sum in the days when a new Ford went for about $400.

The reason he went to jail, of course, was that there was no miraculous investing going on. There was no investing at all, let alone any of the supernatural kind. Ponzi simply took the money from the later suckers and gave it to the earlier suckers, which attracted more suckers. As long as he could attract more suckers, he could continue the payments.

The problem is that there are a limited number of suckers in the world, not because there is necessarily a true dichotomy between the foolish and the wise, but because there are only so many people. Eventually, the con man runs out of marks.

Now, the idea, of course, is that the con man should not wait until the demand for idiots exceeds the supply; before the base of the financial pyramid collapses, the fraud should invest in a one-way ticket to Rio de Janeiro. The criminal gets away with most of the money; the people at the top of the pyramid, who are the early investors, get their money back; and most of the people lose their shirts.

The unfortunate flaw in Ponzi's plan was its timing: someone in the nether regions of the pyramid finally realized what was going on and put an untimely end to this miracle of investing before Ponzi could sail for Brazil.

You can usually find a lot of people who are stupid, but you can't count on them staying stupid forever. The financial charlatan should get out before his victims get an education. Ponzi was just a tad late.

Not too late, mind you, to continue defrauding people: when Ponzi went to prison, people were still writing him *at the prison*—sending him their life savings to "invest." Some people really should live with their parents all their lives.

These stock fraud people are huge criminals, but police never go after them. You have to rely on other agencies.

Instead, the police chase after small-time crooks like the Murphy Man.

But from the police point of view, that can be pretty interesting.

This particular Murphy Man could have been the President of large corporation, or even the President of the United States. He was great.

He used to check the newspapers for the departure times of ships that were in port, and then he would go to bars that catered to sailors. After striking up a conversation with a sailor, he would find out what ship the sailor was on, and that way he would know how long the sailor would be in town. If the sailor was going to ship out within a day, he would make his offer.

His method was to take out of his pocket several pictures of naked women, and inform the sailor that he was trying to arrange customers for them for the night. The sailor would choose one of the women, and pay money to the Murphy Man. The Murphy

Man, a professional in every way, had pre-printed receipts. The receipt said, "Pacific Talent Scouts. _____ [name of customer] has paid $_____ in cash to the Management and is entitled to one ___ regular fuck / ___ blow job [check one] from _____ [name of prostitute]. This ticket must be used on the following date: _____. NO RAIN CHECKS."

The sailor was then given the receipt and told to go to a certain hotel, and stand in front of a certain room, where he would be met by the girl. The girl, of course, never showed up, for the simple reason that there never was any girl at all, and the Murphy Man would simply disappear with the money until the sailor's ship had left for the Pacific.

This man was a great salesman, and could have made a fortune in any legitimate business. He would have been Vice President of Sales of any corporation he chose in no time at all. But he chose this particular line of work, and he made a good living at it.

The reason he was so good at it was that he understood completely why it is that people believe things. People believe things because they want to believe things that are to their advantage. We want to believe that a politician is a good man, or that a corporation will make us money, or that a car is being sold to us after having been thoroughly checked out by a competent mechanic at the dealership, or that we are getting the best price, or that a good-looking person will make a wonderful spouse. That is why we believe lies. We want them to be true. And so, everything the Murphy Man said was something that he knew his victims wanted to believe. People believed Ponzi could make them money because they wanted a magic investment. People believe politicians because they want to believe that the world can be put in order, and the government can make them rich.

The Murphy Man was so good that one time he sold imaginary women to three sailors, from the same ship, but for some reason his victims' ship did not sail when it was supposed to. The next day, when he went back into the same bar, there were the sailors. The sailors, of course, were ready to tear him apart. He did not panic at all. He went up to them and said, "Thank God you're here! I am so sorry for what happened. I was arrested, and the police took all my money, and the women were arrested too. I just got out of jail, but the women are still in jail. I tell you what, I'll make it up to you as best I can. I can't give you those same women, but here are some other women you can choose from, and although I'll have to ask you for some more money for these women, I won't take my cut from it, which is 25%." So he produced new photographs, had the sailors choose three more nonexistent women, took their money, gave them new receipts, and left town until their ship sailed.

One of the sailors was so convinced that this Murphy Man was for real, that he stayed all night long in front of that hotel room, and only left at six in the morning so that he could get back to his ship before it sailed.

End of the Line

It was a call of an 802, a dead person. This one was inside a train tunnel in the Potrero. I drove to the scene and was met by an officer. She looked pale in the moonlight, but even more pale than the moonlight should make her seem. She told me, "It's not good, Sarge. Better be prepared."

It will never do for police officers to vomit all over the evidence at a death scene, or to pass out, or to panic. It's especially important for leaders of people in any emergency to act as if nothing disturbs them. I always admired naval officers who stood on deck, as undisturbed as Zen masters, in the midst of battle, hands clasped behind their backs, calmly issuing orders. I have a photograph of my grandfather, a World War I naval officer, standing just that way, and indeed, his icy command in battle saved the lives of thousands of men.

So before I went to a scene of chaos and grief, I always tried to put myself mentally in a state of calm, and to think of something else, something that would put me in a serene mood. I always wanted my troops to think that nothing could upset me, and that whatever problems arose, I would have the solution.

So I said to the officer, "I'm sure I've seen worse," but except for one time some years later when I saw a cannibalism, this was just about the worst thing I ever did see.

I went down a steep hill and into the dark train tunnel. I was concerned that the trains were not going to travel through the tunnel with people standing around in it, so before I entered, I talked to a railroad policeman who was already on the scene, and he made sure that the trains would not come while I was there..

Walking into the tunnel was like following Virgil into the entrance of Hell.

As we strode into cavern, the darkness ate up the illumination from our flashlights. I strained to see the horror inside.

On one side of the tracks, I saw fresh bloody meat, small chunks of it, with little bits of clothing and hair. The trail of bloody meat stretched down the track for fifty yards. Evidently, someone had been hit by a train, and had gotten caught up in the wheels, so with every rotation of the wheels, another part of that person been cut off and crushed under the weight of the locomotive. There was a sickly sweet smell in the air from the blood.

I came upon another officer, looking quite ill, and I instructed the first officer to take him outside the tunnel for a breath of fresh air.

When they left, I was alone in the blackness of the tunnel. I walked down the tracks; my shoes pressing on the gravel underfoot made a crunching sound that echoed off the walls. I saw two fingers by the tracks, but those were the only remains that were recognizably human, other than hair. They were a woman's fingers, with manicured nails, painted red.

At such times, to keep my composure, I kept my thoughts on other things, and acted as if I were only watching a movie, while still doing my police duty. This dissociation helped me do my duties without the interruption of the emotional reaction I would otherwise have.

The thing that I kept the point of my intellect on was the death of Socrates.

I thought of what Socrates said about suicide in Plato's *Phaedo*. He was against it; he said that we should imagine what our reaction would be if we had an animal such as an ox or an ass, and instead of doing what we wanted, it killed itself. If we could, wouldn't we punish that rebellious animal? If we were God who made people to accomplish our own purposes, and they refused by killing themselves, we would be angry with them.

But then Socrates had to drink the hemlock, and he died.

I found a plastic bag, with a paper in it.

I kept my consciousness on Socrates.

Reading Socrates' conversations in Plato always made me feel like a schoolchild in the presence of my betters, almost afraid to talk. Socrates taught Plato, who talked Aristotle, who taught Alexander the Great, who taught the world to adopt Greek civilization. But who was it that taught Socrates? The wealth of intellect Greece possessed was incredible. How could one little nation be so fortunate as to have such huge minds all at once?

As the Jews say, "Steel sharpens steel; scholars sharpen scholars."

I opened the plastic bag.

So, who taught Socrates? Who started this chain of intellectual explosions that reached such critical mass?

It was Diotima of Mantinea.

I took out a paper from the plastic bag.

Diotima started this intellectual atomic reaction. Diotima taught Socrates about love. Diotima said love is the mediating thing between wealth and poverty. It is love that is the bridge between yes and no, existence and nonexistence; it is love that holds the universe together.

I held my flashlight on the paper.

But most people have never heard of Diotima. Diotima was a priestess—a woman. People think there are no great female philosophers, but they are wrong. The prophetess Diotima started the greatest intellectual explosion in history by teaching Socrates about love. Her discussion of it with him is recorded in Plato's dialogue *Symposium,* and I know plenty of obscure philosophy professors who would give both of their testicles to have that honor happen to them.

When you read of the gentle conversation between Diotima and Socrates, you see that Diotima is really Socrates' intellectual mother. "Hush, now," she says to him, at one point, like a mother to an errant child. We have records of some of Socrates' devastating cross-examinations. But there is no debating with Diotima. She teaches like a mother.

Earlier philosophers wanted to find the unifying principle of the universe, like Thales, who thought, "Everything is water." But Diotima had no such ridiculous notions.

She knew that the universe is glued together by love. She taught Socrates that love is an important part of philosophy.

I read the paper, standing there in that hellish tunnel amidst all of that gore, and I kept my consciousness on philosophy.

Diotima could not have known that the efforts she made to teach a short, stout, ugly man about love, would start something that still resounds thousands of years later. We can perhaps control our actions, but we cannot control the consequences of our actions. Diotima's actions had wonderful consequences.

But the actions of the woman who was torn to pieces by the train did not have wonderful consequences.

The paper was a suicide note. This wretched woman wrote that she had breast cancer, and she had endured two mastectomies, and radiation, and chemotherapy. But her cancer had come back, and had metastasized, and instead of enduring any more therapy or a lingering death, she decided to spare her family the expense of her treatment by killing herself. She had wanted to spare people, but avenging fate decreed otherwise, like a Greek Nemesis who pursues those who defy the gods. If, as Socrates suggested, God would be angry that his creature killed herself, it was predictable that the events she put in motion in her act of *hubris* would frustrate her plans. People would suffer because of her suicide instead of being relieved by it.

Diotima knew the universe is held together by love, but this poor woman's universe came apart in a dark train tunnel, where she died, alone, with no one to hold her as she passed the Veil, no one to speak loving words of comfort to her, and her death hurt the family she wanted to spare and even the unfortunate who was driving the train.

In the lonely tunnel's blackness, I wondered whether she went to heaven or to hell.

It used to be that people did their best to punish suicides after their death, to deter others from following them. They were buried at a crossroads with a stake through their heart, and denied a Christian burial. Now, we realize the people who are depressed aren't thinking rationally, and we now have effective ways to treat depression. Doctors can prescribe antidepressant medication that lets the sunshine into a person's dark world, and psychiatrists have cognitive therapy to correct the bad thinking that leads to depression and suicide.

But some of the old attitudes linger on. I know a widow whose husband blew his brains out with a .38. When she went to her pastor, the pastor told her she couldn't bury him out of his church because her husband was a suicide. A day later, he called her to say he had changed his mind, but by then she had already turned Protestant, and she never set foot inside a Catholic church again. Because I know some of that Pharisee's secret sins, nothing he said could have affected me at all, but he hurt her terribly.

I trudged out of the train tunnel, the suicide note in my hand, taking care not to step on the pieces of this pathetic woman's body.

Poor Diotima was denied her just fame because she was only a woman. People think great philosophers were exclusively men, but it's not true. You don't need a penis to think. A lot of guys try to think with their penis, but that usually ends badly.

Diotima knew that love was something different, something important. Diotima knew that love is the glue that holds the universe together.

Diotima's work bore fruit, far more than she could have anticipated.

I came out of the tunnel, and met the two officers. "She wanted to spare people any trouble over her death," I told them, and handed them the note.

The train had stopped at the next station. Police were interviewing the engineer. I drove to the station.

She had wanted to spare others trouble over her death, but she could not have anticipated the consequences of her actions.

The engineer had been unaware that his train had killed someone until the police told him. He had killed a woman, and he took it very badly. She had destroyed him. When I arrived, he was weeping uncontrollably.

Then he knelt on the ground by his locomotive, and threw up.

Sic Transit Gloria Mundi

In the 1960s, when she was a young topless dancer, she was famous throughout the land for having silicone put in her breasts. In those days, silicone implants had not yet been invented, so she had liquid silicone injected by a large hypodermic needle right into her breasts. It must have been very painful, but she wanted to be a star. And being a star was important to her.

Broadway has a lot of strip joints, and publicists worked hard to keep her in the news. The San Francisco *Chronicle* at that time was the sort of newspaper that ran photographs of brides-to-be in brief bikinis, and the arrival of silicone-enhanced topless dancers was given a great deal of attention.

The nightclub where she worked put a large cartoon drawing of her on its marquee, with her vital parts outlined in neon lights, and large red, flashing light bulbs where her nipples would be.

It was definitely a cutting-edge enhancement to San Francisco's culture.

Tour buses made regular stops at the nightclub, and people all over the country knew of her.

Several decades later, a policeman I worked with had a little ritual. I saw him perform it in the locker room before we went out on patrol.

In his locker, he kept some love letters from this woman, and he silently read them, and smelled them. I guess she had sprayed perfume on them. Then he looked at a large picture of her, standing on the street next to him. She was dressed in frumpy clothes, and he was in uniform. He was a thin man, handsome, with a carefully trimmed mustache and jet black hair. She was blonde, good-looking, but not remarkable in her street clothes. Unless you knew who she was, you would never guess her profession. After that, he kissed the picture, and he was ready to go on patrol.

This ritual was repeated every time he went to work.

We discussed his relationship with her a couple of times. He saw her frequently. He very obviously loved her.

I asked him why he didn't just marry her, if she made him happy.

"Oh, I couldn't do that," he said.

"Why not?"

"It wouldn't work out."

I never found out the reason why he didn't think it would work out. I hate to see people who want something in life not get it because of hesitation and self-doubt. Many people are on the outside of life looking in, like people who press their faces against the window-glass of a restaurant, looking at the people dining and enjoying themselves inside. Too often, people never let themselves go into life's feast.

We very often construct our own prisons, and for no good reason. Why not just decide to be happy?

But the policeman felt, ultimately, that she would not make him happy, and I thought that, too, might be wisdom.

Cops have a lot of contact with whores and strippers, and once in a while, there is a romance. Most of the time, the love-sick cop's buddies talk him out of tying the knot with such a woman, but every so often, a policeman decides to marry one. Sometimes it turns out OK, but it usually, it is a huge mistake, just like you'd expect.

A lot of guys are under the hallucination, fed by Hollywood, that whores and strippers like sex more than normal women. They think that life with such a woman would be spent constantly shaking the sheets. It isn't true.

Most prostitutes don't even *like* sex. They have had so many degrading and painful experiences that sex for them becomes merely something to be endured, and a reminder of past traumas. Women become prostitutes mainly because they cannot find any other way to make enough money, and the usual reason they need a lot of money is to buy dope. Most whores are dope addicts. Many are psychotic.

Strippers are sometimes prostitutes, but with the added psychiatric burden of a strong streak of exhibitionism.

Our society treats male and female exhibitionists quite differently. Male exhibitionists are put in prison, and female exhibitionists are put on stage.

Exhibitionism is a sexual dysfunction, and people who marry exhibitionists quickly find that they are incapable of a normal, fulfilling sex life. Beauty contestants, for instance, have a very high divorce rate. Their exhibitionism, narcissism, and sexual dysfunction ruins marriage after marriage. As my father used to tell me, "Many a man fell in love with a dimple, and made the mistake of marrying the whole girl."

Male exhibitionists generally fall into two categories: those who expose themselves to adult women, and those who expose themselves to little girls. They almost never do it to both. The ones who do it to little girls are the ones who are not confident of themselves with women.

Lily waivers like to see the shock it gives their victims. It makes them feel powerful. Weenie waggers who do it to grown women have sometimes committed suicide after a woman says, "Is that all you've got?"

The act of exhibitionism may be the result of a compulsion. In the Police Academy, we were taught that these guys will do it at a certain time or place, and it doesn't matter if a cop is right next to them. They are compelled to do it.

I didn't believe it. But sure enough, a few months later, I was standing at Fourth and Market when some guy went into a trance within ten feet of me, dropped his pants, and waved his pecker at passing women.

I was very insulted. I felt that he was ignoring my authority. But the fact is, he was just a complete sack of nuts. I arrested him, and the jail psychiatric staff shipped him off to a mental hospital.

Female exhibitionists may become strippers, or they may find more socially acceptable ways of getting attention. They crave attention, and they will do anything they can to get it. They want to be a star more than anything in the world.

It is certainly not uncommon for young women to want to be a star. But most women are grounded enough in the real world that they will refuse to take their clothes off in front of crowds of hollering strangers.

Guys easily get stupid ideas about being in love with exhibitionist women, and it almost always ends badly. Guys think that if a woman advertises that much, there must be something great about her. They think she must be a very libidinous woman. But it isn't necessarily so. Like one of the cops who worked with me said, "They might be dressed in a 'come catch me, come fuck me' outfit, but they don't really mean it."

It's like franchise restaurants: the cheap burger joints spend millions on advertising, and clowns, and marketing gimmicks, but when you finally get served, all you get is a cheap meal with a burger that has so much soy filler in it they're not legally allowed to even call it a hamburger. They have to call it a "superburger" or something else, and put mayonnaise and catsup on it to hide the cheap taste.

Fine restaurants don't spend millions on advertising. They don't have to. You pay extra for a good steak, but you get a good steak.

Women are the same way: the better women don't have to advertise. You don't see the better women prancing down the street in the clothes prostitutes wear. They get quite enough attention without that kind of advertising.

Some guys, of course, can't tell the difference, which is why franchise burger joints remain in business.

You can make a pleasant home with almost anyone, provided they are of good character. This means someone who is kind to you. It means they are loyal. It means they are respectful enough that they don't say mean things to you or criticize you so cruelly that you start thinking bad thoughts about yourself. It means someone who is concerned about you, who will care for you when you get sick. It means someone who will say sweet words to lift your spirits when you're down. It means someone who is there for you when you need them. Such a person has good character, and even if they have shortcomings, you can usually be happy with them.

Someone of bad character will always make you miserable. It doesn't matter how good-looking or rich they are. It's better to be alone than with a hurtful, selfish spouse. That's why Hollywood stars are always divorcing each other. When you look for someone to spend your life with, character is really the most important thing.

When I was 18, just out of high school, I fell in love with a girl of great intelligence, outstanding beauty, and an unfortunate histrionic personality disorder. She kept that particular defect hidden at first—or perhaps I was just not sensitive to it. But when it became evident, it caused me all kinds of grief. Her life was a continual self-centered crisis.

Previously, I had thought that if you love someone, you should try to overcome every obstacle. But this young woman was so mean, that I finally realized that you can love someone who will not make you happy. It was a very valuable lesson, and I was later glad that I learned it when I was only 18.

The policeman who loved the topless dancer was well-aware that you can love someone who will not make you happy. He loved her intensely, and she loved him, and she was always very kind to him—but he knew that she could not, ultimately, make him happy. I suspected that he wanted her to give up working as a stripper, but she didn't want to do it because she was a star, and she had always wanted to be a star.

Eventually, the policeman retired, and moved away.

The topless dancer worked at the nightclub for a total of several decades, which was really an extraordinarily long career for such a performer. Most strippers are through by the time they are thirty. Eventually, the nightclub management decided they needed someone younger, despite her fame, and they fired her.

She had been working well past the time when she could perhaps even have had grandchildren old enough to be working as strippers alongside her, but there are, in this brutal world, limits to everything. At some point, the show is over, and you have to take your curtain call.

I heard of her recently from a cop at Central Station. He said he had seen her driving down Broadway in a beat-up old car. Someone on the street recognized her and shouted her name.

She was delighted to be recognized. Her face completely lit up, and she waved enthusiastically.

When you are a star, people recognize you on the street.

Cain and Abel

His life had changed when his brother hit him on the head with a claw hammer.

He survived, but the claws had gone into his brain, and from that moment on, he was no longer the same.

We never did find out the cause of the fight with his brother. Brothers and sisters can be our second selves, both our closest love and our strongest competitor for our parents' love. We can be very close to them, but when we fight, it is the worst of fights. Our closest family members give us the most intense love, and the most acid hate. That is why a civil war is almost always the most vicious of wars.

But by the time he had descended into the alcoholism that brought him to daily contact with police, the dispute with his brother was over. But things in his family would never be the same again.

I knew him well, and so did every other policeman at Taraval Station. He was the only person I ever knew who had a pre-made booking card stapled onto the wall above the booking counter of the station. The booking Sergeant only had to look on the wall to see his name, his date of birth, his home address, and other identifying information.

He was booked into Taraval Station for drunk every single day.

One year, he was booked in as a drunk 366 times. On one day, someone let him out of jail before 2 a.m., when the bars close down, and he was able to buy liquor, so he was booked twice.

He didn't actually drink more than one or two beers at a time, but the medicine he had to take for his seizures acted with the alcohol to make him as drunk as anyone who had consumed a whole bottle of whiskey.

Every evening, we would go to the 7-11 on Taraval, and he would be passed out, leaning against the building. Every evening, we took him to the station, booked him in, and let him sleep it off.

He was a nice guy when he was sober, but he was horrible when he was drunk: angry, abusive, and very difficult to control. He was only about five and a half feet tall, with a very red face and brown hair, and even though he was slender, he could put up a struggle when he was arrested. All the cops treated him with respect, however, because his reputation as a race car mechanic was one we admired.

His father was dead. His mother had taken out a court restraining order against him, and she had him arrested now and then when he wouldn't leave her property. But she also frequently let him onto her property to do chores for her and get a meal. His relationship with his mother was always a matter of some undefined difficulty.

His brother had served about a year in jail for the assault.

Before his brother whacked him with the claw hammer, he had been a hot rod mechanic, and he had made very good money constructing and selling custom hot rods. He had been much in demand both for body work and for engine work, and he also built engines for race cars.

This was a business requiring intelligence, skill, knowledge, hard work, and creativity, and he had them all. But all of that vanished at the points of his brother's hammer claws.

In those days, it was considered inhumane to put drunks into the county jail for a few months, as had been the practice when I first went into police work. Drunkenness was considered to be a medical and a social problem, so the drunks never went to jail for more than a few hours. The result, of course, was that alcoholics on the street lived a much shorter life, because when they were in the rages of an alcoholic bend, they had no interest at all in any kind of rehabilitation.

And so it came, one day, that we went to pick him up from the wall at the 7-11 food store, and found that he was dead.

We had the coroner pick up his body, and then we went to his mother's house, to tell her.

It was not anything I expected.

His mother took the news quite calmly. "I've known this would happen, some day," she said. She seemed almost cold about it.

We expressed regret that he had died.

"He was a different person, in the old days," she told us. Then she invited us to see his work—two hot rods he had made, just before his injury.

She led us into her garage, and there, parked on the concrete floor, were two of the most beautiful automobiles I have ever seen.

One was a red Ford, and the other a green Plymouth. Both had a deep, lustrous paint job that meant that he had spray painted them, and then hand-rubbed them with fine pumice, and then repeated the process about thirty times. Both had custom body work, done with a care and an artist's eye that meant that the dead man had been a true creative master. Each had an engine that had been entirely chromed, and reworked, with a supercharger and racing accessories that must have caused a fortune.

"I guess I'll have to sell them," she said. "It'll good to be rid of them."

She said it without any emotion or sentiment at all, as if she were talking about the creations of someone else's son. It was obvious that his passing was not about to be mourned for long. We were all created from dust, and to dust we shall return, as God said in his curse of Adam. But it seemed that this man's time on the planet was even more ephemeral than most.

On the way out of the house, we saw his brother, throwing wood and trash onto a fire in the living room hearth. He looked at us calmly, as unperturbed as a cat.

When we returned to the station, the pre-made booking card had already been pulled down from the station wall.

Minotaur

He was a handsome, muscular policeman with thick black hair, and a pleasant demeanor, even if he was a little shy. He loved to arrest criminals, and to write speeding tickets, and to solve crimes. But all of that changed the night he encountered a burglar.

He was working under my command that night; I was a Sergeant, but since the Lieutenant had the night off, I was watch commander. I liked that, because it meant I got Lieutenant's pay. I knew how to do my superior's job.

But this night, I earned every bit of the extra pay, and I wished that I had called in sick.

The call came over as I was holding the lineup. Lineup is when the watch commander gives the officers their assignments, reads to them the bulletins of recent crimes, and does a little training in an often fruitless attempt to impart some of the Lieutenant's knowledge and experience to cops who probably weren't even born when the Lieutenant became a policeman.

Shortly after lineup began, a call came over that the burglar alarm at a high school was ringing, so I sent this cop out of lineup to the school.

He arrived at the school, found an open door, and went in.

There are three main ways to handle the search for a burglar in a large building. In all three, you surround the building, and send someone in.

My very strong preference is to have a police dog and its handler do it. The dog goes by smell, and he is not usually fooled. And if the dog gets shot by the burglar, as occasionally happens, although we feel terrible about it, the dead cop is a dog, not a human being. When I referred to the dogs as cops, I mean it. But they are still animals, not people.

The second way to search a large building is to send in several officers. That way, if there is a big fight, the officers have help at hand. The disadvantage is that more people make more noise, and sound is a principal way of detecting the suspect. The biggest disadvantage is that sometimes cops shoot each other by mistake.

If I have to go into a building, I prefer to do it alone. I go in, gun in one hand and flashlight in the other, and stand stock still, without even breathing, taking in every sensory bit of information I can. I have caught many burglars because I could hear them breathing. There is a mystical sense you have that something else is in a room with you.

As a rookie, I learned to carry a flashlight, even during the daytime, when I went to a burglary on Sotelo Avenue. We had just passed the house, and it was fine. We knew the owners were on vacation. Two minutes later we passed by again, and the front door was open. We went in, and we knew immediately that the place had been hit by a burglar: the furnishings were scattered all over in a search for valuables.

We searched the house, and I went into a huge walk-in closet. It was pitch dark, and I had no flashlight. I waited quietly, sensing the air, and I knew something else was in the room with me. As my vision became adjusted to the dark, I saw a pair of eyes—which jumped out at me, and I nearly shot the house cat.

From then on, I always carried a flashlight, day or night.

It can be quite frightening to search a dark building; you never know what you will find there. A building search is like a trip into your unconscious: you confront dark fears, just as Theseus did in the Labyrinth, or Ulysses, Aeneas and Dante did in their trips to the underworld.

I always felt like Theseus searching for the Minotaur in the black caverns of the Labyrinth. Perhaps you do not find a half-human, half-bull monster in the building you search.

But sometimes, you find something just as frightening.

Sometimes, you find death.

The high school is a huge building that stretches for blocks amid sheltering trees. The policeman walked into its dark, cavernous depths, looking for the burglar.

He came to a candy machine that had been smashed open. The burglar could not get to the armored change locker inside the machine, but he had taken the candy.

The policeman walked on, and then, without warning, from behind a door, out stepped the burglar, gun in hand, pointing it at the policeman.

The policeman fired his pistol, and the burglar dropped his gun and collapsed onto the floor.

When the burglar's gun hit the floor, it broke in two. It was not a real gun—it was a plastic replica, made to look just like a real weapon.

The burglar was a teenager.

I went into the school. An ambulance crew had put the burglar on a stretcher, and was putting an IV needle into his arm. His shirt was off. I saw a little red hole in his chest. He was awake, and moving his head.

I looked down at the burglar's gun. If it weren't broken, I could not have known, from two feet away, that it wasn't real.

I hoped that the burglar wouldn't die, but it was not to be.

The policeman was standing in a stairwell, looking very pale.

I wondered why the burglar had a toy gun. Why would anyone point a toy gun at a policeman? I figured that he thought that he could get the policeman to drop his gun, and the burglar could get away.

In the movies, criminals who point guns at cops get the cops to drop their guns. In the movies, criminals who point guns at innocent people get the cops to drop their guns. In the movies, the cops throw away their guns all the time.

That is in the movies. In real life, cops don't *ever* drop their guns. There was once an incident where a cop dropped his gun because the criminal had a gun on the cop's partner. Once both cops were disarmed, they were both killed. The incident was made into a book and a movie called *The Onion Field,* and police all over America studied that case. Now, a suspect could point his pistol at the President, and the cops still would not drop their guns.

Here was a kid who was living in a dream world.

In some ways, we all make our own reality. We imagine the universe to be a certain way, and it becomes that way. It's not just whether it's happy or sad, but reality bends to our perceptions. People treat us the way we teach them to treat us. The world of *things* may be changed by our thoughts, too. Heisenberg and some of the new philosophers who combine things like quantum physics and mysticism, people like Fritjof Capra and Carl Jung, talk about the observer changing what is observed just by the act of observation. It is wisdom, though, to know what your imagination hasn't changed about your environment, and that teenage burglar's plastic gun didn't change anything about the policeman—at least, nothing that the burglar wanted to change. The policeman took the kid's imaginary gun as reality, and acted on it. It was very bad.

As Richard Feynman said, "Nature cannot be fooled."

The teenage burglar's mother was, naturally, quite upset, and complained long and hard that the policeman had shot her son. The media picked up on the complaints, and then professional cop-haters called for the officer to be punished because he shot a kid "just because the kid was stealing candy with a toy gun." It was terribly unfair, but there was nothing the policeman could do about it.

We expected that. We didn't say anything when the newspapers picked up her complaints, because the mother of someone who was killed has a certain freedom to say anything she wants.

She gets a free pass because she's a mother.

The trauma of having killed a teenager, and reading bitter criticism in the press, had a bad effect on the policeman.

He became terribly depressed. He no longer wanted to talk to people, or to make arrests. Nobody could cheer him up.

Eventually, he found a job in the crime lab, where he didn't have to go on patrol anymore.

Nigger Lover

He was a very tall man, at least four or five inches taller than I was, thin but very muscular. He had thick black eyebrows that overshadowed his eyes like thunderclouds. He had the uneasy gait of Frankenstein and the serious, dark expression of Boris Karloff.

His family was from the South, and he bore the surname of a famous Confederate general, his ancestor, who was well-known for superhuman courage, combined with a bull-headed and disastrous preference for direct confrontation with the enemy, even when he was outnumbered. As a result, he lost a critical battle, and his army with it. His ancestor had none of the flexibility in combat for which the rest of the rebel generals were known.

This policeman was regarded by other cops in the station as a rather dangerous fellow. We had several ghetto areas to patrol, and we had very little community support. It was quite common for us to have rocks or bottles thrown at us when we drove through the projects, and we were often the target of sniper attacks. It was important to most of us to improve relations with the community, even though, in those days before "community policing" became a popular theory, we could not adequately articulate a strategy to bridge the gap between us. But we knew at least that it was important not to mistreat people.

There were about 110 policeman in the station, of whom four were openly racist. They wanted to show dominance over the community we served, whom they regarded as subhuman, whereas the rest of us just wanted to get along. This policeman was openly racist.

He was proud of his Confederate heritage, and put a Stars and Bars sticker on the rear window of his personal truck.

I have long been of the opinion that the Stars and Bars, like the Swastika, is a symbol of people who thought they were better than other people, who were enemies of the Republic, and who treated other people in the worst possible way. The heirs of the liberty that was purchased at so high a cost by the fallen heroes of the Republic, should be ashamed to display the symbols of their enemies.

I was assigned to ride in a patrol car with this officer, on a stormy night.

At about four in the morning, we came upon an elderly black woman, standing at a bus stop on Third Street. We were stopped for a red light, and she tapped on the driver's side window. The officer was driving. He rolled down the window.

Out of the pouring rain, the old lady said, "I live about two miles away, and the buses don't seem to be working. Can you give me a ride?"

It seemed to be a reasonable request. We had absolutely nothing else to do. Nothing at all was going on that required police attention.

But the officer immediately flew into a rage, shouting at the old lady: "You fucking lazy nigger, do you think this is a taxicab? Walk home!" He stomped on the accelerator, and we drove off.

I thought he was angry enough to become violent. "Hey, I need to go to the station," I told him, and when we arrived at the station, I told the Lieutenant that I didn't want to ride with that man another minute.

It is not regarded as a positive thing when officers cannot be put in a radio car together, and this was the only occasion in my career in which I made such a request. I explained to the Lieutenant what had happened, and the Lieutenant granted my request. Then he spoke to the officer in his office, with the door closed. I don't know what was said, but when he came out, the officer was even angrier than when he went in.

In a way, I felt sorry for him. He was consumed by hate.

Hate rots you inside, and love heals you.

After the Second World War, there were a lot of orphans. No matter how clean the orphanage, a tremendous number of them just died. Finally, doctors realized that if a baby is not loved and held, the baby just gives up on life and dies.

You only learn to love because someone showed you love. If you can show your children love, and teach them to love, you are a success as a parent. A child who is loved, and who loves, can do tremendous things of which an unloved child is incapable.

In the Thirteenth Century, the Holy Roman Emperor Frederick II performed an experiment. He wanted to find out what the natural language of people is. He took orphans, and raised them with specially-trained foster mothers, with orders that they get no language or love or stimulation. He wanted to find out what language they would speak—Latin, Greek, German, or something else—if nobody spoke to them. Instead, the babies all died.

Frederick thought the experiment was a failure.

He was wrong. The experiment was a success.

Frederick got his answer, but he didn't recognize it. The language we all must speak first is love.

I wondered whether this officer was ever properly loved. You only learn to love by being loved.

Much later, this officer and his regular partner were fired, which was not a common thing. They had no support from most of the other cops in the station, because we needed to get along with the community, and racist cops who went around abusing people didn't let us do that.

Many years later, he spent time in and out of mental hospitals, and he was arrested for assault. The last I heard of him was when I saw a mug shot of him on a wall at police headquarters, with a warning that he had recently been threatening police.

I don't know whether his mental illness led to his hatred, or whether his hatred led to his mental illness. I do know they were linked.

It was difficult enough for white boys to adjust to ghetto culture, and it made it even more difficult if fellow cops went around stirring things up.

We made friends in the neighborhood, and they helped us get to know black culture. For instance, two wonderful ladies who ran the Everett and Jones Barbeque on Third Street introduced us first to soul food, and once we were properly addicted to it, they introduced us to various other aspects of African-American culture.

The racist cop went up to me after his talk to the Lieutenant. He put his face right next to mine and he said, "You know what you are? You're nothing but a God-damned nigger lover."

"Nigger lover" was the chant a lot of Southerners used when civil rights workers tried to integrate schools. The natural response of any child to being called a name is to deny whatever it is that the child is being called. Part of a correct response to being called a name is to rise up above your childish responses, and to exercise some adult control over the situation.

My response to him caused him to recoil as if I had slapped him in the face.

People in societies where everyone is armed are normally exceedingly polite to each other, and that includes police. In the olden days, when people walked around carrying swords, courtesies were quite formal. You didn't want to start a fight with an armed man. It is very unusual for police to treat each other rudely.

My response was a little use of truth as a weapon.

Gandhi and Martin Luther King used a principle called "satyagraha" in successfully overturning injustices. *Satyagraha* is basically using truth as a confrontational weapon. You don't resist people, but you don't let them bully you. You insist on the truth, you know the truth, you live the truth, and you don't cooperate with evil in any way.

People often do not recognize truth, but police throughout the country have now gone through extensive training to recognize it.

When Lee Harvey Oswald was photographed after his arrest, his face was black and blue. The Dallas cops had worked him over. That was their usual practice, and when they got the biggest case of anybody's career, that's the way they handled it. They couldn't get a confession. They didn't know how. So they beat him.

When the courts stepped in and said they weren't putting up with forced confessions anymore, a lot of cops thought they'd never be able to prove a case again.

But that isn't so. Now, police are trained to recognize truth, and falsehood, and to extract truth from a suspect just by letting him talk.

The basic idea is that when you tell a lie, you feel anxiety, so you try not to tell a complete lie. Suppose, for instance, that you ask a child molester, "Did you molest that child?" And you receive as an answer, "I would never do anything to harm the child." The suspect has shifted to the subjunctive tense, which puts him out of reality right away. He is answering a different question than was asked, answering it with a hypothetical answer—you didn't ask if he *harmed* the child—you asked if he *molested* the child. The truthful answer would have been "Yes" or "No."

In *satyagraha*, you tell the truth: yes, or no. You confront injustice and say, "This is wrong."

Truth is powerful. Truth stands unadorned. It is only a lie that needs a big, distracting, overwrought argument. "The lady protests too much, methinks," as Shakespeare said in *Hamlet*.

I had to laugh when some academic nerds said Martin Luther King's doctoral thesis on *satyagraha* didn't footnote sources correctly, so it was, by implication, a phony thesis, or plagiarized, and that he didn't really deserve his doctorate. In the last century, only a few people were really able to make *satyagraha* work: King, Gandhi, Walesa, Mandela, and perhaps a few others. But make it work they did, and they changed the world. It was a laughable demonstration of our fraudulent academic system that anyone could criticize King, who understood *satyagraha* like no other American, because he was sloppy with footnotes.

I was not going to put up with this officer's bad behavior.

I have never felt the need to adjust my thinking to conform to popular opinion. I hold to some theories that are not commonly accepted, and I reject some notions that most people hold almost without thinking.

One notion I reject is that of race. I do not believe in race. It is not merely that I do not believe in racial discrimination; I do not believe that there is, in reality, such a thing as race. I grant that some people look different from me, but I do not grant that it constitutes a valid classification called "race."

Race is a social concept, not a biological concept. It is not scientific, because it is not well-defined. What race is, and who is in which race, is so flexible a judgment as to be scientifically useless. For instance, Margaret Sanger, the founder of Planned Parenthood, thought that "the Irish race" was an inferior one, good only for manual labor. I don't know what the Irish "race" is. Maybe she meant those guys from Dublin, who always seem to be running around, racing up and down all day, not like my people, from County Cork.

My own family is as multicolored as the United Nations. It didn't start out that way, but all's well that ends well.

So when the racist cop snarled at me, "You're nothing but a God-damned nigger lover," I used a little *satyagraha*, and it instantly defeated him. He had to walk away.

I said, "That's right."

Eyewitness

He was a rotund, elderly man, and he had been a policeman for almost fifty years.

There are a number of career decisions a policeman has to make. The first is whether to be a cop at all, and with which police department.

Later, when the cop reaches fifty years old, he has to decide whether to retire with a short pension or to stick it out to get a full retirement.

For most police, those last few years can be the hardest. Police work is a young person's job. The job eats at you like acid, and it is wise to get out of the business before the acid eats to the bone.

But there are some people who love the job so much, they'd do it for free. If you continue to work past the time when you qualify for a maximum retirement, you're working for pennies on the dollar.

That didn't bother him. He enjoyed the work, the adventure, and most especially the companionship of other cops. Most cops like each other.

As for me, since I retired, I sometimes miss the people I worked with. I don't miss the job at all. I've had enough adventure and enough danger to last several lifetimes. Police work is generally either very routine, or very exciting. And when it gets exciting, it can be just scary. I've had quite enough of it.

But he didn't have enough of it, and he stayed on the job for fifty years.

A quite unique incident happened to him when a man in South San Francisco pulled a bank job, and the FBI arrested him. The suspect was taken to San Francisco to appear in Federal Court.

Bank robbery is not a smart crime. There is lots of security in the bank, there are cameras, the FBI investigates it, and you don't even get that much money. Usually, you get more money knocking over a busy saloon on a Sunday night, when the bartender still has the weekend's receipts because the banks won't open until Monday morning. And the money you get from robbing a bank often has a radio in it to broadcast your location to the cops, and red dye that explodes all over you. It's not a bright thing to rob a bank.

The FBI booked the robbery suspect into the prison over police headquarters, and they wanted to do a lineup. The suspect was a rotund, elderly man.

So, where would the FBI get other rotund, elderly men to fill out the lineup? From the police detective bureau, of course. You don't see too many prisoners of that description, because by the time a man gets on in years, his testosterone levels have usually declined enough that he won't do really stupid things like robbing a bank.

Testosterone subtracts fifty IQ points from your mind, easily.

The FBI asked the policeman to put on an orange jail jumpsuit, and join the lineup. He complied.

Six elderly, rotund guys trudged out in front of the grid of lines marked for height: 5', 5'6, 6', and so on. Spotlights were on them, and the bank teller who had been robbed was behind the one-way mirror.

The bank teller immediately pointed to the policeman, and said, "That's him, that's the man who robbed me, I'd know him anywhere."

People who do not deal with witnesses for a living do not understand that eyewitness testimony is often very weak, and quite often mistaken. You would think that a witness who had been robbed inside a well-lit bank would be able to identify the suspect. Mostly, they can, but very often, they make mistakes.

It has to do with the way we think. We get a certain amount of sensory input, and we imagine connections between things that we think are true. Sometimes we are right, but often we are wrong. We forget things that sometimes we used to know, and we fill in the forgotten blanks with our imaginations. It happens to everybody. It doesn't mean that people are lying; it just means that they are mistaken.

Fortunately, at the time that the bank was been robbed, the policeman had been in court testifying, and the FBI thought that was a pretty good alibi.

But that doesn't mean that it was over for the policeman. Cops constantly rib each other, and this was just too good to be passed up.

Criminal lineups are photographed, and his fellow detectives got the photograph of the policeman in his orange jail jumpsuit. The photograph was prominently displayed in the Sex Crimes Bureau, where the policeman worked.

Every time people came by the Sex Crimes Bureau, they ribbed the policeman about the bank robbery. He heard people ask, "Pull any more bank jobs lately?" every day until he retired.

Surprise

It was the neighbors who called us, because they could hear screaming and thumping in the one-room cheap apartment. Normally, people in the cheap, filthy apartment buildings in the poorer sections of town mind their own business, and do not call the cops, because once the cops leave, the person they called about may be angry enough to kill them. But this time, they called, and that is how we came to save the wife's life.

He was a very large man, about thirty, a truck driver, well over six feet tall, and muscular. He was dressed in blue jeans and, appropriately enough, a "wife-beater" undershirt. His wife's blood was splattered all over the front of his undershirt.

His wife was at least a foot shorter, and a hundred pounds lighter than he was, with a long black hair full of blood, a face covered with blood, and wearing a blue bathrobe, likewise full of blood.

We put handcuffs on the husband, and then asked what had happened.

What had happened was that the honeymoon was over, apparently permanently.

They had been deeply in love, and had married about six months before. The bride had explained to him that she had a delicate female condition, and needed surgery to correct it, but that in the meantime, they could do other things, like oral sex, but they couldn't actually have intercourse until she was well.

And that was all right with him, because he was deeply in love, and no sacrifice was too great for his beloved bride. He even started driving a dynamite truck, because the extra hazard pay meant they could save for the surgery so much faster, and he was willing to risk death so that his bride could someday be well.

Shakespeare said of one woman, "When my love swears that she is made of truth, I do believe her, though I know she lies." And that is the essence of many men's relationship with women. Women hold out to us the promise of happiness, of love, and they represent to us things that we want to believe. Why do people believe lies and other ridiculous things? Because they want them to be true.

Often, we project onto other people all of our hopes and dreams. How many times have we seen some poor fool, smitten beyond reason with someone who could not possibly be as good as he believes? It is because he projects the deepest needs of his psyche onto her, as if he were a movie projectionist in a theater, projecting a movie onto a blank screen. Sometimes, people eventually come to see the reality of the blank screen beyond their projection–and sometimes they spend their whole lives in a state of self–created delusion.

Women are sometimes especially artful at using themselves as a blank canvas, painting themselves new faces and creating new persona. And men are often more than enthusiastic in accepting the reality of that painted picture.

Women just run circles around men's minds. They grab hold of our imaginations, and lead us as they might lead a bull with the ring in its nose. Men are even unaware that women are using makeup to create the new persona.

When I was in high school, about 16 years old, I took a girl to a dance. We doubled–dated with one of her classmates and her classmate's boyfriend. I will never forget that dance.

My date's friend seemed to be one of the most beautiful girls on the planet. She had huge, soft eyelashes. I had never seen a girl with such wonderful eyelashes. When I shook hands with her, I noticed that she had well-formed, long fingernails. Her figure was far more womanly than any other girls my age. I was enchanted.

I might have been warned about the situation a little better if I had paid attention when the girls wanted to show themselves off to their teachers, but I was oblivious to what was happening. They attended a convent high school for girls, and we stopped off at the convent. Two teachers came out, and one of the nuns actually didn't recognize her own student—my date's friend. We say, socially, that we don't recognize someone who is looking very good or very bad, but in this case, it was literally true. The teacher was incredulous of the fact that this beautiful girl was the same student she had seen in class all year. I thought that the nun must be going blind. No one could possibly fail to recognize such a beautiful girl.

We went to a restaurant for dinner, and there a horrible thing happened. One of the girl's fingernails fell off. I thought it must be painful, but she was not only beautiful, she was very brave–she didn't cry at all. She just put it back on. I didn't understand it. If one of my fingernails had fallen off, I would be wincing with pain. And I certainly didn't think that I could have pulled off one of my fingernails and then just put it back on. I had never seen anyone lose a fingernail before. I wondered what caused it.

Then, while we were eating the soup, one of her huge eyelashes fell in the soup bowl–the whole eyelash, not just a hair. I was getting alarmed. This girl was falling apart right before my very eyes.

While we were eating the main course, she lost another fingernail. By now, I knew this was serious.

I knew that there was only one explanation for this.

This poor girl obviously had leprosy.

Since I was a child, I had been told of Jesus healing the lepers, and how lepers' fingers and other body parts fell off. I had never met a real live leper before, and I was shocked to think of how such a beautiful, brave girl could have such a terrible disease.

I was more susceptible to thinking that this was leprosy than the average 16-year-old boy because the previous semester, I had been assigned by a teacher to read a biography of Damien the Leper for a book report, and its lurid accounts of the suffering of lepers had a profound effect on my already over-active juvenile imagination. I became quite frightened–obsessed, actually–with the possibility of contracting leprosy, to the extent that when I was introduced to people who had lost a finger in an accident, I tried not to shake hands, just to avoid the possibility that it was really leprosy, and not a table saw, that took the missing digit.   The concept that there was a contagious disease that could cause people to leave fingers, toes, ears and noses on the ground behind them as they walked, like kids dropping gum wrappers on the street, appealed to my adolescent sense of horror. The book had left me quite shaken.

She offered to pass me the salt, but I refused. I didn't want any of the leprosy germs that might be on the salt shaker. I didn't mention to her that I knew her terrible secret.

Then I recalled with dread that I had shaken hands with her. I was in a panic. I had leprosy germs on my hand, and when I had eaten, I had spread them to my face!

I excused myself and went to the bathroom. I looked at my face in the mirror—the face of a leper. I imagined what I would look like in a few weeks when my nose fell off.

I washed my hands vigorously, and then my face.

I went back to dinner, taking care to avoid any contact with the girl, or anything she touched.

I knew you couldn't cure leprosy. Only Jesus could, and he wasn't going to the dance. I was miserable, but I acted like I was having a good time.

A little later, the other girl and her boyfriend went to the bathroom, and I used the opportunity to mention to my date that I thought the girl might be gravely ill. My date laughed and said it was just her false fingernails and false eyelashes falling off.

I was humiliated beyond words. I couldn't believe I was so naïve, and I was very displeased with the other girl for what I regarded as simple deception.

As miserable as I was about my lesson in artificially enhanced female pulchritude, I was even more unhappy when I told my mother the story of the girl with leprosy.

My mother thought it was so funny she almost gagged from laughing.

Then she had a long talk with me about girls, and false eyelashes, and false fingernails, and false character. My mother is not a false person. I just expected that all the other members of the distaff side were like my mother, and, evidently, that was not the case. I suppose that it is a big part of growing up to realize that not all women are like your mother, and that can be both a good thing and a bad thing.

I thought it's fine to have lipstick and eyeliner, but if you become totally unrecognizable with all that war paint, somewhere there is a line that has been crossed from enhancement to deception. It was a dance, not a Halloween party.

And it was the deception that made me upset. I didn't like being fooled.

Today, forty years later, I wouldn't have a reaction like that—not that women have changed, but that I am a little more able to recognize such things as false eyelashes. They may or may not enhance a woman's face, but I am generally not deceived as to whether they are being used. It is the deception that is key. Back then, when I was 16, it was different. Since my mother never used false eyelashes and false fingernails, I had no idea that they were even part of a regular woman's armory. I had been completely fooled. I was only about sixteen, but I suppose I should have been a little more sophisticated. I just didn't think any girl I knew would resort to such things, and I wanted to believe, against the evidence, that this girl was really that beautiful.

I thought false eyelashes and fingernails were like cheating at cards. You think this girl is beautiful, with hypnotic eyes, and they're just glued on. It's not fair. It is taking unfair advantage of the fact that a man's brain freezes in the presence of beauty.

In the war between the sexes, this is like using nuclear weapons.

And when my mother said that some women put cotton in their bras, I was stunned. I thought that should be definitely against the law.

Obviously, I had even more to learn about women than I had to learn about medicine.

After that, I regarded girls with a little more caution–and a lot more awe. I hadn't realized they could transform themselves into such a completely different person.

And I owed an apology to the nun who couldn't recognize her student. Some time later, I again met that same girl, without her makeup, and I didn't recognize her, either.

The truck driver and his wife told their stories.

The marriage was very happy for about six months, with the bride keeping house in their tiny apartment, and the husband driving a truck full of explosives, and the two of them saving for the operation. They both looked forward to the wonderful night when they could have regular sex after her operation.

But this night, the husband had been drinking with some of his friends, and when he came home, quite loaded, he was not to be denied. Operation or not, he was going to consummate the marriage, then and there. He tore off his wife's dress, and stood looking at her, for the first time, stark naked. He then discovered why his wife had always been so modest that he had never seen her without at least some clothes on.

He looked at his bride for a long time, not comprehending the situation.

His wife had beautiful long black hair, and a wonderfully full bosom, and a pecker the size of a Texas Longhorn bull. As every cowboy knows, the horns aren't the only long thing about a Texas Longhorn bull.

Finally, he realized that he had married a transsexual, a man whose sex change operation was only partly complete; he had received the hormones and the breast implants, but not the rest of the operation. The husband realized he was married to another man–and the fight was on.

We had him handcuffed, and they were both crying.

Through his tears, the husband asked me, "Does this mean I'm a homosexual?"

I felt like asking him, "How the hell do I know if you're a homosexual, you twit? If *you* don't know, why should anybody else know?" But I didn't ask him that.

Here was a man, older than myself, asking me if he was a homosexual. You get a lot of weird questions like that in police work. People think the badge makes you an authority on everything.

I didn't feel qualified to answer him–but I knew that it was this question that held the key to domestic war and peace. If the wife had transformed him into a homosexual, he might think he should kill her–if "her" is the right word to use. This is the basis of a lot of violence toward homosexuals; people think gays have the magic power to transform others into homosexuals, by a touch, or even a look, and they think, unconsciously, that they have to defend their manhood. They think that if a gay man looks at them crossways, or especially if he flirts with them, it must be that the gay man recognizes that they are homosexual underneath it all, and they have to defend themselves. They think that homosexuality is like some kind of supernatural spell that gays can cast upon you, and then you'd turn away from women forever.

So I stepped right up to the plate. Psychiatric help 5¢, the doctor is *in*.

"No," I said with as much authority as I could muster, "It doesn't mean you're homosexual. It just means you didn't know what you were doing. It'll be OK."

He might have been driving a dynamite truck, but he certainly didn't have dynamite for brains. But, given the glass house of my prior naiveté with women, I thought I shouldn't throw any stones.

He was relieved. "That's OK, then?" he asked. They both stopped crying, and the wife was looking hopeful.

"Sure," I said. "It happens to lots of guys. You didn't know what you were doing. Don't worry about it." And indeed, it does happen to lots of guys. Quite a few sailors have had a good time with a girl who wasn't, and they never even found out.

The wife said she didn't want to press charges, and so we released the husband.

Then we left them alone, to sort out their suddenly very complicated lives.

Choice

Of all the crimes I ever saw, the coldest and cruelest was one a man did to his own mother.

We were called to her cheap basement apartment on a burglary. The place had very little furniture, but a great deal of the detritus of medical care: half-used medicine bottles, prescription advisory reforms, pamphlets from hospice on how to deal with dying, plastic bedpans, and other cheerless items we use at the end of our lives.

She was a woman of about fifty, of average height, but no flesh at all. She looked like a skeleton with skin. I doubted whether she could have weighed ninety pounds. Her hair was thin–almost nonexistent. Her eyes were surrounded by black circles. She had metastatic cancer.

After her chemotherapy and radiation failed to stop her cancer, she came home to die. She had a nurse from hospice coming in to check on her every few days. She had used her last few dollars to buy a large bottle of pain medication that her doctor had prescribed. But now the bottle was gone, she had no more pain medication, and no more money, and with every hour, her pain was becoming increasingly unbearable.

She knew who stole her pain medication: her son.

Her son was a narcotics addict.

She didn't call the police; a social worker had. She didn't want to make a police report, because it would mean sending her son to jail.

The degree to which a narcotic enslaves a user is not appreciated by normal people. The narcotic first gives them a rush of happiness and fulfillment. The total body reaction some people get from a first smell and taste of fine wine in which they feel a salivation and a warm rush all over is to the first experience of narcotics as a rhesus monkey is to King Kong. Before long, separating the user from the narcotic will not only stop the warm, happy rush–it will cause incredible pain, like a thousand needles pressed into the user's skin, and then electrified. Withdrawing from narcotics "cold turkey" can make an addict so sick he can die.

The narcotic also numbs the user's ability to think. It destroys his reason, blocks his emotions, and turns him into a zombie whose every waking moment is filled with the craving for the narcotic. Nothing is too dangerous, nor too degrading, no crime too serious, no act too vile, for the narcotic user who needs a new hit of dope. Girls–and boys–who should be enjoying high school are turned into prostitutes, used by diseased old men and left back on the streets–all to feed their addictions.

The walls of Park Station, which covers the Haight-Ashbury district, are covered with pathetic pictures and wanted posters. The wanted posters are put out by the parents of runaway children who have come to San Francisco to escape conflicts at home, hoping to come to Haight Street and wear flowers in their hair, and feel the love. But they find that the only way to survive is to live the drug–addled life of the teenage whore.

There is one girl whose mug shots are on the wall, whose progression from runaway beauty to drug–ravaged hag is classic. Her mug shots, from her arrests, are spaced a few months apart. Her first arrests showed a fresh–faced, beautiful young blonde of twenty, arrested for drugs and, of course, prostitution. Each progressive mug shot, taken a few months later, showed that she stopped washing her hair, stopped wearing makeup, and stopped eating anything healthy. After about three years, she looked fifty, with sunken eyes, and an expression that could have come from a zombie in a horror movie.

The complete command that narcotics have over the minds and lives of addicts is not something that has any twin in the lives of ordinary people. Only the parent of a newborn baby comes even close to the complete dedication narcotics demand: if anything threatened your baby, there is nothing you wouldn't do, no sacrifice you wouldn't make, no fight you would consider too hopeless, no labor too hard. Nature makes parents that way, to protect their children. Narcotics wires that into the addict, in an evil mirror of a parent's love.

This wretched, dying woman's son had condemned her to die in agony by taking her pain medication. And in doing so, he didn't think of his mother. He didn't think of being arrested. He didn't even think of himself: he only saw narcotics, and he was compelled to take the bottle. He didn't have a choice.

"He's the only family I have," she said.

She had borne him out of wedlock, and her family, embarrassed by the pregnancy, had thrown her out of the house. "I made my choice," she said, "And they wouldn't hear of it." She spent the rest of her life in poverty.

Choice. No other word has as powerful an influence on people.

Choice. What is a choice? We speak of "the right to choose," but it is hardly ever true. Women aren't given any real choice. They are given a choice of, "Do this, or else." That's not a choice. That's just a dilemma.

We like to pretend that women have "choice." But it's a lie. If we punish one decision or another, it's not choice, any more than it's a choice if I stick a gun in your ribs and say, "Your money or your life."

So women either bear the child, and we impoverish them and ostracize them, or they get the abortion, and we ostracize them for that, and call them names. In later years, no matter what their decision, when they look back with regret upon their lives, we treat them with disdain. We want them to take it without complaining, since they are "liberated."

We tell women, quite falsely, that they have a choice, and that is our excuse to treat them as if they weren't even human.

If you don't think women suffer because of these things, you simply haven't been listening to any women. They suffer, all right–all their lives. They see someone who is the same age as the child they might have had, and they secretly wonder what that child would look like, and how it would be if they had a family.

We have neither sympathy, nor any kindness for them, because we like to maintain the illusion that what they did, they did in a free choice. We insensitively demand that they shouldn't be upset about it.

It is a cruel joke to pretend that women have a choice. We give them no support, and no options, and then we say they have a choice. You might as well say that women choose to obey the law of gravity when you throw them out of a window.

The pain we inflict on women cannot be alleviated by any known medication.

There was a notorious case, after the Second World War, which attracted the attention of ethicists.

A woman was detained in a postwar concentration camp, and her husband and children were on the outside. She was going to have to wait two years before she could leave the camp, but one of the guards told her that if she would sleep with him, he would let her go. She slept with him, and rejoined her family. Her husband knew–and approved–of what she did, and her family welcomed her.

The question for the ethicists was, did this woman do the right thing, or not?

To me, it is clear that this woman was raped. She was blameless. She didn't have a choice. The guard forced her to have sex with him by threatening to keep her imprisoned for two years. He might as well have held a knife to her throat. A woman with a knife to her throat does not choose to have sex. It is a dilemma, not a choice.

We'd like to imagine that we have choice, that we have complete control over our lives. But in reality, our ability to exercise control is very limited, and every new choice becomes limited by previous choices. We do not choose when to be born, or to whom, or where; we are male or female without anyone asking which we would prefer–and the same applies to our race, our nationality, our intelligence, and whether we are good-looking or ugly. People certainly treat us differently because of those things, over which we have no control at all.

We think we are sailing our own ship, the captain of our soul, but we are really carried along by the hurricane of impersonal fate.

What little control over our lives that we do have is gained with difficulty, and is easily lost. Nothing destroys that control more quickly and more thoroughly than dope. Narcotics addiction is slavery.

The wretched woman was sitting on a chair, too sad to even weep.

"Really, officer, he didn't have a choice. Please don't arrest him," she pleaded. We took the report, but we told her we were going to arrest him anyway. It was our job, and we had to do it. It was one more loss of control for this dying woman.

We called an ambulance to take her to a hospital in the hopes that they could give her pain medication there. "We're sorry this happened to you," we said. "But he can't be allowed to do that to you."

This poor woman had suffered because she brought her son into the world, and now, as she was about to leave this world, her son ensured that she would suffer even more. It wasn't fair.

But she remained loyal to him, and even now, asked us not to take action against the son she loved.

"Oh, he doesn't have any choice any more about these things," she replied. "Don't feel sorry for me. Of the two of us, I'm the lucky one."

Oedipus

For more than thirty years, I have remembered that night, and I know that if I live another thirty, I will still remember the man who died in my arms, stabbed to death by his own son, while his wife looked coldly on.

We got a call of a family fight in the projects on top of Hunter's Point hill.

The projects were ground zero of a nuclear meltdown of crime, poverty, ignorance and hopelessness. They had been built during the Second World War as temporary housing for shipyard workers, and after the War, they were converted to housing for welfare recipients.

There was not a supermarket within a three mile radius, because crimes such as shoplifting and armed robbery were so high, no supermarket could make a profit. The residents had to shop in little grocery stores where they paid prices that were at least half again as high as everyone else paid. There were very few jobs, little of the accouterments of learning such as libraries, few restaurants—life was quite dreary.

It was also dangerous. The leading cause of death for young people in the Hunter's Point projects was murder.

Before I worked as a rookie cop in those projects, I had never in my life been in a home in which there were no books, no newspapers, no telephone, and sometimes even no mirrors.

I found the lack of books to be particularly depressing, because it meant that the occupants were not even thinking of self-improvement. They had simply given up.

This particular home was better furnished than some. It had a sofa of a cheap quality, and two matching chairs, with clear plastic covers over the sofa and chairs to preserve them from dirt. There was a carpet on the floor. The carpet was full of blood.

On the carpet, when we arrived, lay a man, the husband and father, a man of about 40, and thin. He had the heavily creased face of a man who is been dealt more than his share of troubles in the poker game of life. He was bleeding from a stab wound to his gut. A large kitchen knife lay beside him.

People think they ought to pull a knife out of their gut if they've been stabbed, but the opposite is true. The largest number of stabbing victims to survive come in to the emergency hospital with a knife still stuck in them. The knife fills the hole, and helps control the bleeding.

The man's son stood about six feet away. He was about twenty, muscular, shirtless, and his hands were covered with his father's blood.

The victim's wife stood a little farther out of the room, motionless. She was a hardened-looking woman. I noted that she neither approached her husband to comfort him, nor did she comfort her son.

We called for an ambulance. We told the ambulance dispatcher that the victim was dying, and to come Code 3—red light and siren.

We spoke to all three of them, and found that the son had been using dope, and his father confronted him about it. The mother didn't think the father should punish their son. The conflict escalated when the father flushed the son's narcotics down the toilet, and his son stabbed him. It was a neighbor who called police.

We called for an estimated time of arrival of the ambulance, and were told it would be there in about five minutes.

We handcuffed the son, and this brought the first reaction from his mother: she said she didn't want him to go to jail. He was a good boy, and she loved him, she told us. We told her we had to do these things, and she went back to her passive stance.

Another five minutes went by, and we asked again where the ambulance was. "Any minute now, they'll be there," was the reply. Our orders were to call an ambulance, not to transport injured people ourselves, or I would have dumped him into the back of my radio car and sped off to General Hospital.

A continual problem with the projects is that the kids in the neighborhood consider it fun to take down the street signs, or even turn them around. They feel that if you don't live there, you shouldn't be there, and they love to confuse outsiders. We figured the ambulance crew was lost.

The man was slipping in and out of consciousness. He said, "I love you" to his son, who said he loved him too, and he said, "I love you" to his wife, who said, "You too," rather coolly.

I knelt by him, propped his head up with one hand, and held his hand with my other. My partner was yelling into his radio for the ambulance to get there, fast. I didn't think it would make a difference at this point whether the ambulance came at all.

Many people have died in my arms. Every time it happens, it drains me, emotionally and spiritually. I feel as if I have given about a quart of blood afterward. But I try to give as much of my spiritual energy to the dying person as I can; I try to project into them as much love, and strength, and happiness as is in me, to give them a little gas in their tank for their journey. Twenty years after this incident, I did the same thing from my own beloved, mortally injured son. But fortunately, I could not see that far into my own dark future.

His breathing was becoming labored. "I'm here for you," I told him. He smiled.

We don't know what happens to someone when they passed the Veil, how they are judged, or what their new life is. But I am certain that we have a soul, and that it continues to live. In thought, there is freedom, and that is not something that anything physical has. Physical things are bound by physical laws, and they have no freedom. It is a soul that causes our free thoughts.

Our soul also causes life. What is the difference between a live body and a dead body? Everything physical that is in a live body is also in a dead body. The cause of life is nonphysical. Since the cause is nonphysical, it is not affected by physical corruption or death. The soul lives on.

I always regarded the moment of death as magic, as sacred. I always tried to make that person's passing as comfortable as I could, even when the surrounding physical circumstances were a complete pandemonium.

He looked up at me and smiled weakly. "It's all right," I said. I felt sorry for him, having to die in the arms of a stranger. His wife did not make a move toward him. I rocked him gently, as if he were a baby.

His eyes fluttered, but he maintained their focus on me. I kissed him on his forehead, and told him that God loves him, and he died.

Someday, if I am fortunate, someone I love will hold me as I enter the next world. I wondered who it will be, and when.

I do not believe that there is such a thing as chance. I do not believe that there are such things as accidents. Everything that happens, occurs because of someone's act, because of someone's will. We attribute to chance things that happen with a cause we cannot see—but everything has a cause.

I was like an obstetrician, aiding his bloody birth to a new life.

I do not think it was by chance that I came to hold that poor man that night as he entered another sphere. For some reason, I was meant to be there, to be his guide and his comforter. I do not know what that reason was, but I know that there was one.

It was an enormous responsibility: this caterpillar became a butterfly, while I held him.

For a minute, there was silence. I stood up, and said a silent prayer.

Then we heard the ambulance arrive—without its red light and siren. The ambulance attendant sauntered in. "What took you so long?" I demanded.

"We had to get gas," the attendant said. I suspected that lunch was also something that took priority over this man's life.

The lives of people in the projects are simply not important to the rest of society. To the ambulance crew, it was just another ghetto stabbing.

The man had died as he had lived: not important to anybody. His dying needs did not change the order of business for the ambulance crew. He died for his son, who murdered him, in an attempt to keep his son away from dope. But no one in his family supported him.

We took the son to the patrol car. On the way, his mother kissed him, and they each said they loved the other.

It was the second murder I had been to that week, within the space of a block.

Tyger! Tyger! burning bright

Leonard Lake's idea was that he would kidnap women, make them his sex slaves, and at the point of his orgasm, kill them so that their death shudder would enhance his climax. He would also kill men for their money, and anyone else who got in his way. He built a soundproof concrete bunker on his remote property at the little mountain town of Wilseyville, in which he and his buddy Charles Ng tortured and killed women in front of his video camera. In all, he killed three women, seven men, and two babies—that we know of. His actions were finally uncovered when he and Ng committed a petty theft in South San Francisco, and he was nabbed. The cop who made the arrest found him with a gun and a silencer, and Lake took a cyanide pill at the booking counter.

The cops went over the videotaped killings. In one, a tearful and frightened woman is pleading for her husband and baby. They were, of course, dead by that time. The woman was later killed, horribly. The other videotapes were even worse.

It is because of such people—and there are quite a few of them around—that the traditional advice cops gave to women changed. In the old days, police told women not to resist. So many sadists now torture and murder their victims that the standard advice is to run, scream for help, and fight like fifty wildcats. Never, ever, let a criminal tie you up or take you somewhere else. The "somewhere else" the criminal wants to take you to is a safe place—safe for him, not for you. Don't get in a car, don't let anyone drive you anywhere. Crash your car into a telephone pole if you're being forced to drive. Resist, lady. Fight, lady. Have a plan, and have a weapon. Pepper spray works very well. Have it in your pocket, not your purse.

The San Francisco police got involved with this horrific criminal pair because the Wilseyville police needed someone to go over some of the evidence, including the videotapes.

We assigned some people to go over the evidence and the videotapes, and then word began filtering out that the people who had the assignments were quite traumatized.

A lot of people are under the impression that human beings are basically good, and they might make mistakes, but if you scratch their surface, you'll find something really good, and if you teach them the right way to act, they'll act that way.

I don't think so. I think that if you scratch most people, you'll find a rat. The only reason most people don't absolutely screw up their lives is that they never get a chance. It is terribly important for us to so adjust social pressures that people are not going to do things like murder you over a parking space.

When I was a kid of maybe 10 or 12, my parents were watching a program on TV. It was something to do with the Holocaust, although at that time that term wasn't yet used for what happened to the Jews. I remember someone saying things about lampshades made out of human skin. When my mother became aware of the fact that I was in the room, she made me leave. She told me that this was not something that I should know about.

That is all that she had to say for me to become very well-informed on the Holocaust. There is hardly anything that anybody ever told me to keep my nose out of that did not cause me to compulsively find out everything I could about it. I went down to the main library and read everything I could about the Holocaust. I went through all of the volumes of *The Trials of the Major War Criminals*. It was as big as an encyclopedia. I didn't read every word, but I did skim through every page. I read Viktor E. Frankl's *Man's Search for Meaning, The Diary of Anne Frank,* and other books. The best book on the subject by far was Frederic Wertham, M.D., *A Sign For Cain.* Wertham discussed the fact that the ovens that were used in Auschwitz and Dachau were first designed and built for use in the German mental hospitals. Highly respected people were involved in these things.

At first, I couldn't understand why people would do things like that.

I talked to everybody I could find who knew about it. I talked to dignified old ladies in fur coats and pearls with numbers tattooed on their arms. I talked to GIs who came back from the war and really didn't want to have to remember seeing things that nobody should ever have to see.

Everybody told me the same story. People who deny the Holocaust are just Flat Earth idiots. Everybody told me the same thing, and none of them knew each other.

Even though I was a kid, I was very sharp. I asked people questions, about all sorts of subjects, and it became kind of an amusement in the neighborhood for the adults to see what questions I could come up with. It was only amusing, of course, if somebody else was being grilled by this little kid. Everybody knows a little kid who seems more like a reincarnated old man, and I was that kind of a kid.

I talked to Frenchmen. I had a lot of knowledge, but of course I only had a kid's social skills, so I didn't realize that I was stepping on people's toes. I asked the Frenchmen I met if they had been in the Resistance during the war. They all gave me a kind of funny look, and said, "Oh, of course, I was in the Resistance. Secretly." I was only a kid, but I knew I was being lied to. Those guys were in the Resistance like I was in the circus: as a spectator. If all the Frenchmen who told me they were in the Resistance had lifted a finger to stop the Germans, Paris would never have been a big rest and recreation stop for the German Army. What does it take to wreck a German troop train? A big wrench to take nuts off the tracks, and the determination and courage to do it.

The Germans had those guys frozen with fear. When I was in Paris, I saw a plaque by a little park. The Gestapo had pulled a dozen people out of a house and shot them right there on the street because they were suspected of being in the Resistance.

That sort of thing kept people from the Resistance. People look out for Number One.

For a long time, I couldn't understand why people would do such a thing as Dachau, and then when I finally understood, I didn't want to read about the Holocaust again. People do it because they want to do it. People like doing it. The guards at Auschwitz who killed babies and cut off women's nipples with gardening shears really loved their work.

It's not just the Germans who would do a thing like that. In this country, we did it to black people, and we did it to the Indians. The Germans had Auschwitz; we had Andersonville. After the Second World War, we ran concentration camps of our own for the defeated soldiers. Between half a million and a million of them died. We don't know how many, because we are Americans, and we don't keep the careful records the Germans did.

The English did it to the Irish, the Spanish did it to the Indians, the Dutch did it to the Africans, and so did the Belgians. Just about everybody did it to somebody.

Every once in a while someone comes up with a suggestion that some class of people shouldn't even be alive, and they cloak themselves with humane weasel words. It usually comes up in the context of medicine. People say, for instance, that we should encourage sick old people to kill themselves. Humanely, of course. Very humanely. People think doctors should be allowed to kill their patients, with or without their patients' active cooperation. Oh, Dr. Wertham, how little we heeded your warnings. We hanged people for this stuff at Nuremberg.

These people were all so *respected*. When John F. Kennedy, Jr. crashed his plane into the Atlantic, there were news reports of how long it had been, and how long someone can survive in water that is of a given temperature. Did you ever wonder how we found that out?

We have that information because in the Second World War, the German air force, the Luftwaffe, wanted to know how long they should look for downed flyers in the ocean. So German doctors put Jews in swimming pools of ice water, and timed them to see how long it took them to die at different temperatures. Those Nazi doctors' research saves hundreds of lives every year. Some of us still disapprove of their methods, but we all enjoy the benefits. Some of the very best doctors and scientists in the entire world were involved in the most hideous Nazi medical experiments.

So, one side says doctors should assist in encouraging sick old people to commit suicide, or to do some other kind of killing. They don't, of course, use the word "kill." They use some euphemism.

Then, in this debate, someone else says we're on the slippery slope to Auschwitz.

I don't think we're on a slippery slope at all. There is no slope. We've gone over a cliff, all of us, the whole world, and those things brushing you in the face are branches you hit as you go down.

We, the heirs of Patrick Henry, now keep people imprisoned, indefinitely, without trial. We run our own Gulag Archipelago around the world. Liberal law professors now debate whether we should have a court sanction torture. Conservatives have never debated it at all. The government listens to our telephone calls and reads our mail. "Give me liberty or give me death" is now replaced by "Give me security." Don't give up your guns; you never know when you might need them very badly.

George Orwell just got the date wrong.

While we debate torture, Muslims debate—*debate,* mind you, because they somehow see two sides to it—whether it was *moral* for Islamic terrorists to send suicide bombers into a Russian school and murder 300 children. The tiny children followed their teachers into the school like little ducklings after their mothers, and the Muslims blew them up. To state it is to condemn it, for anyone who is not an evil lunatic. But this weary world has no shortage at all of evil lunatics. I don't know what kind of a religion it is where that sort of thing is debatable. Maybe I just don't know enough about religion.

The whole world falls apart; the center cannot hold.

When we land, having gone over the cliff, we may at least have the comfort of knowing that we are not alone, that someone has been here before. We may be able to look up from the spot where we hit bottom and see above us the sign in the beautiful wrought iron gates to our new homeland—the old lie, *"Arbeit Macht Frei."*

I know a lot of people get very angry when you suggest that the Holocaust was not a unique event. I don't mean to offend anyone. But the fact is that the evil in people's hearts that caused the Holocaust is not unique to goose-stepping Germans. I guarantee that if you built an Auschwitz in California, I could get Americans who would want to run it.

Maybe I don't know as much about philosophy or history or literature as I'd like to know. But there is one thing that I do know far too much of, and that is what the old radio show *The Shadow* referred to as "what evil lurks in the hearts of men." I know lots about that, far more than I'd like to know. And what I know of that tells me that it is a very dangerous thing indeed to start selecting other human beings to die.

Sometimes you have to do it; sometimes you are forced to do it. But don't let anybody tell you that it won't come with a price, or that the price won't be high. The evil in our hearts, especially our desire to erase other people from this planet, is a tiger we keep in a cage, and that tiger is always hungry. We let that tiger out of its cage at our peril. We always think that it would be a good thing if someone *else* were erased, if someone *else* were eaten by the tiger, but once that tiger is on the loose, it's just a question of who's next.

We all have a dark side, and to read these words without understanding that there is evil in every single one of us, is to be merely entertained without any insight at all.

People say, "But a *doctor* will be in charge," as if that is any kind of guarantee of ethics at all. Maybe a committee of doctors will make these decisions. Much of the world's medical research is done in Africa, where people don't know what's being done to them. This is going on right now, today. *"Paging Dr. Mengele."* The tiger is loosed upon the world.

Civilization is a thin sheepskin cloak over the tiger. At the beginning of World War Two, a British commander was shocked at those who wanted to bomb factories in the Black Forest. "Are you aware that is *private property?*" he asked. But such moral restraint did not last long. By the end of the war, the British were killing 135,000 innocent refugees, burning them to death in two days of fire-bombing in Dresden, purely a civilian target, just to show those awful people a lesson they'd never forget. We'll all be safe in *this* slaughterhouse, Kurt.

We love violence. We love to see people get hurt.

We all have Leonard Lake's heart.

We are entertained by violence, all right, and that is the most important thing. Our entertainment is more violent than anything since ancient Rome. We will pay for that. We dissemble and deny that it's harmful, especially to our children. But we will reap a harvest of blood.

Even the most representative poets of our age, W. B. Yeats and T. S. Eliot, have the darkest of muses. They have put their ashen marks upon our foreheads. We live in a self-created eon of loveless, unending night.

People like to think of the Holocaust as a unique event, and in certain ways, of course, it *is* unique. But it is also very depressingly common. "Never again" is a great motto, but it is already false, a dozen times false. It is a goal, and a necessary goal. But no one should imagine that our technical advancement is reflected in any way in moral advancements in our souls.

I saw one of the men to whom the assignment had been given to go over the evidence and videotapes of Leonard Lake, on his way home after work.

He came out of the elevator door to the basement garage in police headquarters. He sat down in the driver's seat of a police car, locked all the doors, covered his face with his hands, and wept.

Killer

He had killed more people than anyone else I ever knew.

His job in Vietnam had been to shoot people with a machine gun mounted on the side of a helicopter.

He enjoyed it.

He liked to shoot people with a machine gun so much that he had signed up for two extra tours of duty in the war zone.

He had killed between two and three hundred people, one at a time.

But then the Vietnam War ended, and he decided to become a policeman.

I didn't know his history when I first met him, but there was a look in his eyes that completely horrified me. It was the cold stare of a rattlesnake.

Normal human beings react emotionally to other people in a way that reflects them. We call it "empathy."

In normal human interaction, our facial expressions change in a way that parallels the expressions of people we are with. If they smile, we smile. That is "rapport." Rapport goes deeper: the brainwave patterns of nursing mothers match those of the infants at their breasts.

But this man did not have empathy for other people, and he made no attempt to establish rapport. If you spoke to him, he looked it you, without any emotional reaction at all. He would reply, and his replies were not *inappropriate*, exactly, but they were the sort of replies you might expect from a robot, if a machine could carry on a conversation.

I suspected that he had been severely traumatized at some point in his life, and of course, I was right. As psychologists say, "Hurt people hurt people."

When you take another human life, something is taken out of your soul. There is a cost to taking human life, any human life, no matter how unworthy, and that cost runs high.

We live in a culture that glorifies killing even more than almost any other culture since ancient Rome. The average child will have seen over 10,000 murders on television before he reaches First Grade. Behavioral psychologists know that it is of no use to say that the child knows that these are not real killings, because the effect on his psyche is entirely the same: a killing is shown, and everyone is happy because of it. Then the child is introduced to video games where he becomes the killer, and he is rewarded for killing. His behavior is shaped by these things.

We wonder why children in our society now do things like gang killings and the Columbine massacre. If an evil scientist had set out to turn our children into a nation of murderers, he could not do better than invent television and video games.

We glorify killing. It is masculine, it is powerful, and it solves problems. We as a people want killings. There are human lives we want snuffed out.

It is false to say that, "Killing is not a solution." Certainly it is a solution. Violence and killings solve all sorts of problems—that is why we resort to them. But every killing comes with a price, and that price is high.

Sometimes, we have to kill. But it is just dishonest to pretend that it doesn't have consequences. Every time we taking human life, there is a terrible cost.

This man was mutilated inside by killing so many people.

I thought he might start killing people as a policeman, but he didn't. But he also didn't heal. He could never relate normally to people. I knew him for many years, and all that time, he still had rattlesnake eyes.

He was finally assigned to a job where he pretended to be a dope dealer, and with his cold look, nobody suspected he wasn't the real thing. Dope dealers kill their customers as a relentlessly as tobacco executives. They have that rattlesnake look, too.

Another man who was almost his opposite wound up killing half a dozen people during his police career.

He was a thin, mousey-looking man, the type that you would expect to see doing computer programming with a plastic pocket protector in his shirt, or serving ice cream sodas, in a white shirt and a polka dot bow tie. He had the look of a complete nerd, of the sort that becomes a caricature in comedy movies. He was also very, very nice to people.

Criminals are predators, like lions, and they are always looking for the easy kill.

Which antelope does a lion kill? The slow, the old, the weak, the helpless.

Human predators are exactly the same. The prey who attracts the attention of the big city's carnivores is the person who shambles alone down the sidewalk, hardly able to walk, let alone defend himself in a fight, and who keeps his eyes downcast because he is too timid to look at others.

Those with a firm, confident walk, especially in the company of friends, looking ahead without staring aggressively, who appear ready to put up a fight, are much less likely to become victims of crime.

The big city predator passes them over, and waits for an easier target.

This short, slender, Casper Milquetoast-looking policeman appeared to the meat-eaters of the city as a wounded gazelle appears to hungry lions.

To them, he appeared to be the sort of person who, when he was a child, other children would tease, and beat him up, and steal his lunch, and throw apple cores at him. He just had that look.

They were very wrong in judging this book by its cover. Dead wrong.

In half a dozen occasions in his life, robbers made the fatal error of going up to him, pointing a gun at him, and demanding his money.

The advantage the robber had over the policeman is that the robber had a gun already pointed at him, and all the robber had to do was squeeze the trigger, whereas the policeman had to draw his weapon, aim, and pull the trigger.

But this advantage is trumped by the fact that the robber expects his victim to pull a wallet out of his pocket, not a gun; and the reaction time necessary to recognize that the black object in his victim's hand is a revolver, not a wallet, means that the policeman can put a shot right between the headlights before the robber can even recognize his peril.

Recognition of the object as a gun takes at least a quarter of a second to half a second; acting on it takes another quarter to half a second. But bringing a gun up from waist level and firing it only takes a quarter to a third of a second, with no recognition time. He who decides to shoot first, and acts quickly on it without hesitation, wins.

Six times, the scene played out with real guns, and six times, the robber was standing on the street with a pistol in his hand, and a .38 slug spinning through his forehead. Six times, "Your money or your life" were the last words the robber ever said —in his life.

Having waltzed this dance of death, time after time, the mild-looking policeman was not exempt from having to pay the piper. The emotional toll it took was high.

Finally, his wife stepped in and demanded that he retire, and that they move to a small town where that sort of thing doesn't happen. She could not take—and she knew he could not take—one more such a confrontation.

And the mild policeman, knowing he was overmatched, complied.

Erased Masterpiece

He was a teenager from the ghetto, and we had arrested him for graffiti. He had drawn a quite beautiful picture of one of his friends, who had been shot dead in a gun fight. He had drawn it on someone's garage door, without permission. The owner of the house, not wishing to get involved with gangsters, declined to press charges. We stood over the artist while he erased his masterpiece by repainting the garage door, and then I had a talk with him.

"You know, this is really good," I said. "Do you take art in school?"

"I'm not in school. I dropped out of school last year."

"Why?"

"I don't need school to do OK."

"Who poured that shit in your ear? Somebody who's going to spend the rest of his life in jail, I'd bet."

"Yeah." He looked a little sheepish.

"Look, if you can draw that way without any training, you can make very good money when you've learned how to do it properly in school. Why don't you go to school for it? Then, when you get to be forty or fifty, you'll have a house and a good job instead of living on the streets."

"Man, I'm never going to be forty or fifty. I'll be dead before then."

One of the most discouraging things in talking to ghetto kids is their feeling that they do not have a long life expectancy. Kids in general have a hard time thinking that they won't be young forever, but ghetto kids are quite fatalistic. They really believe they'll be dead long before middle age.

If you'll be dead before you're twenty, a lot of other decisions, decisions that would seem very ill-advised in a normal kid, make perfect sense. Why go to school, if you'll never live to full adulthood? If you're going to die tomorrow, why do your math homework? A date with death in the near future means that you should live for the moment.

If you want to convince a ghetto kid that he should get an education, you first have to convince him that he'll live long enough to use it. And with his friends getting killed every day, that can be a tall order.

"All your friends dropped out?" I asked.

"Yeah, I'd be the only one in school."

I looked at him. I wasn't sure if it was any use talking to him, but I decided to try.

Like any good salesman who has an unanswerable objection, I changed the subject. "You know, you can be like everybody else, or you can be an individual. There's nothing shameful about either choice, but you have to understand that it is a choice, and you're going to pay for it either way. If you want to be like everybody else, you're going to give up your individuality. If you decide to be an individual, you're not going to fit in as well. You can't do both. You know, you have the chance to have real success. But if you want to be a success, you'll have to be an individual, and quit the gang. I think you have the guts to do that. It takes courage. Otherwise, you'll never have a good life. I look at you I can tell from a block away that you're a gang member, and I know what gang you're in."

"Yeah, and I know what gang *you're* in," he said.

"That's true, I'm in the blue gang. But you know, among other policeman I'm regarded as quite a unique individual. They're a little afraid of me. They don't know what I'll do next.

"You have to choose. Do you want to be like everybody else, or do you want to stand out? You can't have it both ways. It takes courage to be your own man. It takes guts to be an individual. It doesn't take any nerve at all to be like everybody else. You are a very good artist, and you could be a great artist. The question is, are you brave enough to do your own thing?"

The surest way to get a teenage boy to do something is to imply that he isn't brave enough to do it. We talked for a while more, and he agreed to meet with a school counselor to get his diploma and move on to art classes at the junior college.

I thought I'd done a pretty good job. Here was a kid with some real potential, an artist who could contribute something of great value to the world. I thought, maybe I've made a change in his life, and he won't turn out so bad after all.

The gang culture of vengeance is very old. For thousands of years, primitive societies had revenge as the prime means of ensuring justice. "An eye for an eye" may leave the whole world blind, but it is the only deterrent against villainy that much of the world has. If there is no effective government, the fact that a crime will be avenged is the only thing that can keep people safe. In ancient times, and in primitive areas today, it was a necessity. We see the tit-for-tat cycle of vengeance in the Middle East and in gangs in America.

The cultures in the Middle East and elsewhere make revenge of family wrongs a matter of honor. Warfare never, ever stops. It goes on for hundreds, even thousands of years.

Some South American Indian tribes almost became extinct because each killing required another. Only the Christian missionaries who told them that they should simply stop and forgive each other, saved them from total annihilation.

Sometimes, love conquers, but often it's only after people are just sick of the killing.

I had doubts at first, but then, to my joy, I found that my efforts were working. Within a week, he dropped by the station and proudly told me that he had signed up to take the classes he needed to graduate—plus an art class. I savored the sweet taste of success. At least one ghetto kid was going to have a fulfilling life, and I had worked the miraculous change. I felt wonderful.

Six days later, a kid in a rival gang shot him dead.

Desperado

I met him when he was trying to get a room in a cheap hotel, a miserable place built a hundred years ago to house impoverished sailors as they waited for the next ship.

He was fifty-two years old, just as old as I was, but he looked seventy. His hair was gray, and his back was bent. He bore the aging marks of prison, of bad prison food and incompetent prison medical care.

He used to have a family, and love, and he took it all for granted, many years ago. He didn't take it for granted any more. He had treated love as less important than money and dope, back when he was young, but he knew better now.

We talked as he waited on a hard bench for the hotel manager to return from lunch.

He had spent the last thirty years in prison, and he had been out five days.

In his hand was a cheap black duffel bag, containing a change of clothes. It, and some cash that he had saved, constituted all the material goods he had in the world.

He had been young, once, and he had enjoyed a good time. He liked alcohol, and he tried drugs. Quickly, the drugs became his life, and then he turned to robbery to support his drug habit.

He robbed a bank, which is never a bright idea. Nothing has more security than a bank.

He used a gun to rob the bank, which is a worse idea. You don't need a gun to rob a bank. There's a kind of an understood, unstated agreement: the robber can go into the bank, give the teller a note, and he'll get money, and nobody gets hurt. There is no need for a gun. The cops will catch him later. They usually do. And then, if you've used a gun, you spend a lot more time in prison.

But he was too drug-addled to think, and he robbed a bank with a gun. He was sent to prison, and he stayed in an eight foot by ten foot cage for thirty years.

This is a hell.

You see people like he used to be, in court. They are young, muscular, confident, with rippling biceps and the confidence of young lions. Whatever life throws at them, they can take it. They are strong, and they are brave.

No matter what they have, they have a hunger for things they can't get, and like young lions everywhere, they think they can just take what they want.

Then the judge hands them a sentence: thirty years in a little iron cage, and they find out that they can fight anyone and win, but they can't fight Father Time. They rot in prison until the testosterone that shut down their brains is gone, and all they have is an old man's body, and they are as mild as lambs.

Standing arrogantly in court, the young lions don't know what is in store for them, but they eventually find out. They stay in prison until they are old, and everyone who knew them is old or dead, and everyone who loved them has either forgotten about them or is on the wrong side of the grass.

Eventually, they get out, to a world that no longer remembers them, and no longer cares.

His mother and father got sick, and he couldn't visit them.

His parents died, and he couldn't attend their funerals.

Like the other young lions, he suffered. After a few years, they come to their senses, and they regret the things they did. They are not the same person any more. But they had been dangerous—more dangerous than any wild animal, and they must still spend an eon in a little iron cage, alone with their suffering, and their hunger for the love they used to have. They spend day after day, hour after miserable hour, with their regret.

His sister died, and he couldn't attend her funeral.

His brother wouldn't talk to him, because he had stolen from his brother to support his dope habit.

He had hoped to be married, but his fiancée left him when he started taking dope.

Other men his age had a wife, and a family, children to love and be loved, and even grandchildren. Children and grandchildren make us immortal: our life lives on in them, even when we are gone. Our love has brought life that lives beyond us.

He had none of that. He had no one to love him, and he would never, ever have children.

Nobody had loved him for thirty years. Prison is a place of punishment and loneliness, not of love. This is a life that is dry as any desert, a life of bitterness and misery.

Now, he was out, hoping to pick up the shattered pieces of his life, to work enough so that he could get Social Security in another ten years so that he wouldn't starve when he grew old, and perhaps, to find love.

He was unfamiliar with love, but he wanted it more than anything. Love is a language. You learn it like you learn any other language: from your mother. Like any other language, you use it, or you lose it. He had forgotten what it is to be loved.

The meaning of life is love. The reason the universe was created was to induce humanity to live, purely and unselfishly, as God loves. Only those who can love, intensely, and purely, can experience life at its fullest. It is a language that is well worth the trouble to learn.

The young lions think they are so strong that they don't need love, but they are wrong. Eventually, they look inside themselves, in their eight by ten hell, and realize that without love, they are miserable. Strength and courage are not substitutes for love. There is no substitute for love.

Love is the most precious thing in the world. Without it, your life is mummified.

The young lions stay in their cages, and realize, eventually, that they aren't getting younger, and their pain drives them down into a deep depression.

He was lonely, and he was unloved, and he was impoverished, and he had a history that would make any right-thinking woman treat him with revulsion.

For $350 a month, which was about a third of the money he had saved from his prison job, he rented a room in the hotel for the month—an eight foot by ten foot room up three flights of stairs.

At last, he was free, legally. But emotionally, he carried his lonely prison with him wherever he walked.

He hoped to find some kind of work, even at minimum wage, and pay into Social Security, and perhaps open the gates to his rocky heart, and let someone love him.

He had learned at least one thing in prison.

You'd better let somebody love you, before it's too late.

Afterword

There are a few comments which should be made upon closing.

The stories in this book are true, all of them. But they are not a history. I wrote the facts down as I remember them happening, or as they were told to me, mainly by other cops or witnesses. With a few exceptions, I did not check them against written records or newspaper accounts. That, I'll leave for historians.

So, for instance, if you want to know if *"Ghost Story"* is true—it is. I wrote it the way it was told to me, by people who had no reason to lie. But if you want to know if there really was a teacher's ghost in the window, or if the schoolchildren were just seeing things, you'll have to make up your own mind. Your opinion on the nature of the actual events is just as good as mine. The only thing I can tell you for sure is that the cops who went there were very, very unsettled by the matter.

Some people want to read police stories with a Mickey Spillane theme: a hardened guy with a .38 under his arm and a whiskey glass on his desk, investigating a leggy dame in stiletto heels with a big chest that hides a heart as cold as a pawnbroker's appraisal. Instead, this book is about the sort of cop who walks through fifty yards of gore and thinks about Socrates while he steps over human body parts. Much of the writing is about philosophy, and theology, and psychology, and such ruminations are there in the hopes of finding some meaning in this ocean of human tears.

This book isn't just about crime. It's about life.

People want to know why I'd write a book like that.

How could I?

It was easy.

There are some themes in the book that may stimulate the desire for further reading, and I hope they do. There were some references I made to theories that may seem a little difficult, at first, and for the interested reader, I include a few sources.

Those who are interested in Carl Jung will do well to start with his classic book, *Man And His Symbols* (New York: Doubleday & Company, Inc., 1964, 1972). Treat yourself to the large hardbound copy, with many helpful color illustrations, not the paperback, which does not have such superb illustrations. The illustrations are important. Don't be cheap. Go ahead, reach into your pocket for the necessary; you'll thank me later. Joseph Campbell, ed., *The Portable Jung* (New York: Penguin Books, 1977) is also excellent. A wonderful movie on some of the same things Jung discusses, more or less, is available on DVD: *What the Bleep Do We Know!?* There is a very good study guide available free at www.whatthebleep.com/guide/ which will be helpful to understanding the movie.

Joseph Campbell also wrote the classic book, *The Hero With A Thousand Faces* (Bollingen Series XVII, Princeton University Press, 1949, 1973). It's about the universal truths of myths, and how they relate to our psyche. If you haven't read it yet, now is the time.

You can read the references I've given, and make up your own mind.

Another theme, and a very dark one, is that of depression and suicide. To be a police officer is to deal with human misery all your professional life. Nobody ever calls the cops because they are happy.

A substance called "serotonin" affects our moods, and when it gets out of control, our moods go down the toilet. There are medicines to correct that now, and if you feel depressed, unhappy, unable to sleep, or unable to get work done, go to a doctor and get some medicine. I strongly recommend going to a psychiatrist. There's no shame in it at all. Nobody even has to know. Why be miserable? Why not be happy?

Your thoughts affect your moods, as well. Bad thoughts, which are almost always in some way untrue, cause bad moods. "Cognitive Therapy," which is a cutting-edge outgrowth of behavioral psychology, is a way of identifying those bad, untrue thoughts and correcting them. Happiness is all about what is going on inside your head. Control that, and you control your moods.

A very good book—no, a *great* book—Dr. David D. Burns, M.D., *The Feeling Good Handbook* (NY: Penguin Putnam, Plume, 1990, 1999) is the best thing I've read on the subject. It actually works. Read this book, follow its advice, and you will become happy. I am not kidding: this stuff can transform you from an unhappy wretch into a joyous person who really does feel good. It will be the best twenty bucks you ever spent. *Why not be happy?*

Jack Young was murdered on August 29, 1971. (That is one fact I did check against the records, just as these words were written. I had forgotten the date.)

I miss Jack, and everyone who knew him misses him, too. He was a wonderful man, and a great policeman.

His bones sweeten the earth wherein he sleeps.

Plato makes good reading.

Diotima had it nailed: the force that holds the universe together is love.

About the Author: Turk Parker is the pen name of a San Francisco cop who now is enjoying his retirement.

Made in the USA
Charleston, SC
08 March 2012